NATURALLY NUTRITIOUS

NATURALLY NUTRITIOUS

Dr. Nicole Kurland

Two Harbors Press
212 3rd Avenue North, Suite 290
Minneapolis, MN 55401
612.455.2293
www.TwoHarborsPress.com

ISBN - 978-1-935097-37-2
ISBN - 1-935097-37-7
LCCN - 2009928968

For more information about *Naturally Nutritious*, log onto **www.thehealthycookbook.com**

For more information about chiropractic care and nutrition, please contact Dr. Nicole and Dr. Jeremy at 1st Choice Chiropractic and Wellness,
2145 E 120th Ave Suite H, Northglenn, CO 80234 and check out their website: **www.turnonyourpower.com**

Food Photography by Candice Albach www.albachstudios.com

Pictured on the front cover clockwise from the top left: Chewy Oat Cookies, Chocolate Oat Jumbles, Everyone's Favorite Chocolate Chip Cookies, Cinnamon Sugar Cookies, Hummus with Baked Tortilla Chips, Goat Cheese and Cranberry Salad with Maple Pecans, Chicken Parmesan

Book sales for North America and international:
Itasca Books, 3501 Highway 100 South, Suite 220
Minneapolis, MN 55416
Phone: 952.345.4488 (toll free 1.800.901.3480)
Fax: 952.920.0541; email to orders@itascabooks.com

Cover Design by Jenni Wheeler
Typeset by James Arneson

Printed in the United States of America

To my beloved husband and 3 wonderful boys. Thank you for your unconditional love and support. I love you all. Thank you to family and friends for testing recipes and to my sister Candice for photographing the food.

CONTENTS

INTRODUCTION

Growing up in Alberta, Canada, I was raised on meat and potatoes --- lots of it. We ate homemade, well-rounded meals and rarely went out to eat. Mom often had a chocolate cake baked and the cookie jar was usually full. Getting dessert was contingent upon having a cleaned dinner plate. My inherited sweet tooth ensured that every morsel of my dinner was consumed. Although I was active, overeating led to my dreaded nickname-- JELLY ROLL.

In high school I became obsessed with dieting and losing weight. My version of healthy eating changed several times during the following decade. I tried all sorts of fad weight loss methods; low-fat, low-carb, artificial sweeteners, over-the-counter diet pills, ephedra drinks, "fat-grabbing" pills, over-exercising, and eliminating meat, dairy, and gluten. Nothing seemed to result in the weight loss that I wanted. I loved food and planned my days around my next meal. My desire to eat and fear of gaining weight led to bulimia, which made my food obsession much worse, damaged my health, and despite my efforts, did not make me lose weight.

It wasn't until I went to chiropractic school that I became educated about true health, and how to achieve it. I started to eat organic --- real food. I eliminated artificial sweeteners, preservatives, chemicals, and fad diet foods, which I replaced with food in its natural state. Instead of focusing on losing weight, I focused on being healthy. I stopped overeating "diet foods" that society told me would miraculously help me drop the pounds and stopped counting calories and grams of fat. I allowed myself to eat fulfilling and satisfying amounts of whatever I wanted and to my surprise, my body actually started wanting healthy foods. I realized how physically awful I felt after eating harmful foods, and how great I felt mentally after releasing my food obsession.

Incorporating foods that increased my energy and improved my health was not difficult to do. Coconut oil, whole grains, stevia, agave nectar, nuts, and seeds became staples in my diet. I eliminated (or drastically reduced) white flour, refined oils, and refined sugar. In addition to feeling better, I really enjoyed the quality and tastes of different foods. I ate when I was hungry and until I was satisfied, and stopped before I was full. Rather than eating mindlessly, I made a conscious decision to stop when the food stopped tasting as good as that first bite. Even though a meal was delicious, I didn't have to finish all of it --- I could save some for the next day or make the same delicious meal again. There was one side effect to my new way of living ---for the first time in my life I was losing weight without even trying.

Instead of an unhealthy obsession, food became a joy. Today, I love healthy, delicious recipes that empower my body. Though I searched for healthy recipes in countless cookbooks, more often than not I found most books only supported aspects of healthy eating. I found no single book that encompassed all of my food philosophies, so I took it upon myself. By experimenting and substituting wholesome foods in existing recipes and making up new recipes, I created nutritious dishes that didn't taste "healthy." I snuck whole wheat pastry flour into my husband's favorite cookie recipe and, to my surprise, he still said they were delicious! My husband, friends, and three beautiful boys became my sounding board for the new recipes that I created. My family and I are healthy and active and I now lead a truly balanced, happy life.

As holistic chiropractors, my husband and I educate our patients about how to improve their overall health by moving more, eating better, and having a well-functioning nervous system. When patients started asking me for healthy (yet tasty) recipes, or a cookbook that I would recommend to buy, I clearly could not confidently recommend any that encompassed my philosophy --- my way of life; however, I realized that I already had a collection of my own recipes. Initially, I intended to produce a small leaflet to share with patients, but I soon realized that my recipe collection was so big that, if I wanted to share it all, I would have to write a cookbook.

NUTRITIOUS BASICS

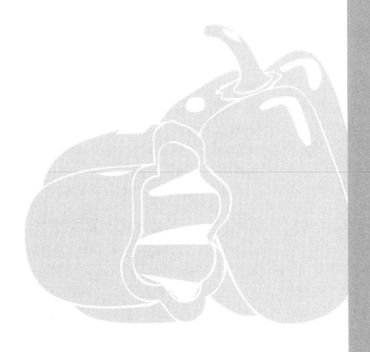

CHAPTER ONE

PLAY WITH YOUR FOOD

Recipes are simply food ideas created out of imagination, taste preference, and availability of products. If you don't like one of the ingredients in a recipe, please feel free to use the original recipe as a guide and make it your own; add or delete seasonings to suit your tastes or, in a main dish recipe, substitute your favorite vegetables for those listed. I have written these recipes to be versatile and easy to follow. Suggestions for substitutions have been given in case you don't have an ingredient on hand; there are no strict rules that a recipe must be followed exactly. The results of a recipe can differ drastically in baked goods because of altitude, type of dry ingredients or fat used, and how much the batter is mixed. If a baked goods recipe doesn't turn out the first time you try it, don't give up on it. Alter the amount of dry or wet ingredients or leavener, and try again.

OILS

Fats are an important part of a healthy diet. The types of fats that you to choose to eat are vital. Whenever possible, avoid refined oils and "partially hydrogenated" oils. The high-heat and chemicals used in the processing of refined oil results in rancidity and oxidation and destroys essential fatty acids (omega-3 and omega-6). Trans-fatty acids are produced when hydrogenated oils are molecularly altered to be more shelf stable. These fats are very dangerous to your health and may cause disease and inflammation.

Essential Fatty Acids (EFA's) are necessary fats that humans cannot synthesize. EFA's must be obtained through diet. Omega-6 fatty acid is abundant in foods in the average diet. It is important to eat some of this essential fat; however, most people ingest too much omega-6 in proportion to Omega-3. Vegetable oils, including sunflower, corn, and safflower oil are high in omega-6 fatty acids. They turn into trans-fats when heated and studies have shown that excessive omega-6 intake can lower your metabolic rate and contribute to hypothyroidism. I encourage you to decrease or eliminate the use of these oils. Omega-3 deficiency is very common in the United States. The ideal ratio of Omega-6 fatty acids to Omega-3 fatty acids is 2:1. Most Americans eat a ratio of 20:1. This imbalance causes damage to your overall health. Omega-3's are found in a variety of foods including flaxseeds and flaxseed oil, hempseeds and hempseed oil, walnuts, pumpkin seeds, salmon, mackerel, avocados, cold-pressed and unrefined canola oil and some dark green leafy vegetables. I recommend including these foods in your diet as well as adding at least 1000 mg of a high quality fish oil supplement to ensure an adequate intake of Omega-3. Look for pharmaceutical grade fish oil to avoid ingesting dangerous mercury and PCB's. Omega-3 fatty acids help to alleviate depression and decrease inflammation while supporting the cardiovascular system, immune system, reproductive system, and nervous system. In general, it can dramatically improve your overall health.

Grapeseed oil is a light, neutral flavored oil that is high in antioxidants, reduces LDL (bad cholesterol) and increases HDL (good cholesterol). It is a very stable oil with a high smoke point which makes it perfect for grilling and sauteing. Grapeseed oil's neutral flavor won't clash with other foods and is great for making salad dressings. It is also beneficial topically for nourishing your skin. When using oil for frying or coating vegetables before seasoning, a little goes a long way. Start with the recommended amount in the recipe. If the ingredients start to stick to the pan, add some cooking spray or more oil (coconut oil, extra virgin olive oil or grapeseed oil) one teaspoon at a time.

Extra Virgin Olive Oil

Extra Virgin Olive Oil is an extremely healthful oil that is high in monounsaturated fat and antioxidants (especially Vitamin E and Vitamin A) and can reduce the risk of heart disease. There are several varieties of olive oil. Extra virgin is the least processed and is extracted from the first pressing of olives. Buy cold pressed oil, because it is extracted without the use of heat and chemicals. Olive oil can be easily oxidized by light and oxygen that can turn the oil rancid. Look for extra virgin olive oil in dark green bottles and store in the fridge or a cool dark place to reduce oxidation damage and preserve freshness. This oil is great for making salad dressings and cooking on low heat. It will solidify in the fridge so, before using, let the bottle sit at room temperature or place in warm water for a few minutes to liquefy.

Coconut Oil

Coconut oil has been maligned for years but is now starting to get well-deserved recognition for its nutritious properties. Coconut oil is an extremely healthy fat that has been used in several areas of the world for hundreds of years. This amazing oil has a variety of uses and health benefits. The addition of coconut oil to your diet can help prevent disease, stabilize blood sugar, increase your metabolic rate, and help you lose weight. It is rich in lauric acid, which is antiviral, antifungal, and antibacterial. It is stable at high temperatures, has a long shelf life, and does not need to be refrigerated. It can be used for baking and frying, and topically to nourish dry skin and help prevent sun damage and wrinkling. Coconut oil does not oxidize, even when heated to high temperatures and it is an antioxidant which helps to fight damaging free radicals.

Coconut oil contains a healing saturated fat called medium-chain fatty acids(MCFA's). Although it is a saturated fat (which frightens many people), it actually helps with weight loss. Medium-chain fatty acids are digested easily and are utilized differently than other fats. Instead of being stored as body fat, the MCFA's in coconut oil are immediately converted to energy, which raises your metabolic rate, and assists in weight loss.

The quality varies greatly among brands you will find, due to the types of coconuts used and the process used to extract the oil. The effectiveness and health benefits will be directly related to the quality. Use coconut oil that is certified organic, unrefined, non-GMO(not genetically modified), not hydrogenated, no "copra" (dried coconuts), and not bleached or deodorized. Good quality coconut oil will have these terms listed on the label.

Small containers can be pricey but this oil will last you a long time and is absolutely worth it for the health benefits it provides. There are several quality brands--three that I like are NOW, Nutiva, and Tropical Traditions. I buy a large container of coconut oil and it takes several months to use up. I highly encourage you to incorporate this amazing oil into your diet and use it topically. Just a tablespoon daily can make a huge difference to your health. Of course, the use of this oil must complement a healthy lifestyle. It will not be as beneficial without eating other healthy foods, exercising on a regular basis, and eliminating harmful foods.

I use coconut oil daily both topically and in food preparation and I firmly believe that it has greatly contributed to my health and my weight loss. The oil's coconut flavor is hidden in baked goods and when used to cook vegetables for sauces, soups and stir-fries. Coconut oil forms hard lumps when mixed directly with cold ingredients. When using coconut oil in baking, stir it with a whisk in a bowl then add the sugar next. Whisk vigorously until creamy then add the wet ingredients. If adding an egg directly to the coconut oil, let the egg sit in warm water for a few minutes to avoid lumps. I have included this amazing oil in my recipes but have also given an alternative if you choose.

Oil Options and Cooking Sprays

Organic butter, cold-pressed and unrefined canola oil, grapeseed oil, and extra virgin olive oil are good options for oils. In my opinion, though, coconut oil and cold-pressed extra virgin olive oil are the two best oils to use on a regular basis. I use cooking spray oil often when cooking. There are a variety of cooking spray oils and some are healthier than others. Choose olive oil cooking spray when using low heat, and grapeseed oil spray when using high heat.

SWEETENERS

Whether you use evaporated cane sugar, brown rice syrup, agave nectar, raw honey, maple syrup, brown sugar, or white table sugar, keep in mind that they are all still sugar and should be used in moderation. I believe that there are many benefits to using a less processed sugar in your diet. Highly processed table sugar is completely stripped of all nutrients and has no nutritional value. Many people are aware that too much sugar can damage a person's health but replacing sugar with artificial sweeteners is not the answer. Chemical sweeteners such as Sucralose(brand name Splenda), Acesulfame-K, Aspartame, and Saccharin all have many reported side effects and, in my opinion, should be completely avoided. Some of the complaints regarding aspartame reported to the FDA include headaches, dizziness, behavioral changes, abdominal cramps, seizures, fibromyalgia symptoms, multiple sclerosis and lupus--to name a few. In animal research studies, a few of the side effects linked to Sucralose were a decrease in the size of the thymus glands, enlargement of the liver and kidneys, and a reduction of red blood cells. If you are trying to lose weight, there is no clear evidence that artificial sweeteners will assist in weight loss. In fact, some evidence suggests that artificial sweeteners can actually stimulate your appetite. Use natural sweeteners such as agave nectar, stevia, evaporated cane sugar, and organic brown sugar or Sucanat, in limited amounts, as alternatives to processed sugar and chemical sweeteners.

Agave Nectar

Agave nectar(also called agave syrup) is a natural liquid sweetener made from the extract of wild agave cactus. It has been cultivated for hundreds of years, first by the Native Americans, then in Europe. It is gaining popularity in the United States due to its many health benefits. It is slightly thinner than honey, dissolves easily (even in cold drinks), has a long shelf life, and will not crystallize. Agave is an unprocessed sweetener. It retains all of the vitamins and minerals that are stripped away from processed sugars. It has a low glycemic index (30) compared to honey (which ranges from 60-80) and table sugar (90). It does not cause a sharp rise or fall in blood sugar and is therefore useful for diabetics and hypoglycemics. Agave nectar has a delicious, sweet taste and is wonderful in countless sweet and savory recipes. Use it to sweeten warm and cold drinks, on pancakes, in baked goods and in sauces--- as a replacement for sugar pretty much any time you need a sweetener. To incorporate agave nectar into your baking and cooking, use the following tips: use 3/4 cup agave for every cup of sugar called for in a recipe, reduce the liquid by 1/3 and decrease the oven temperature by 25 degrees to prevent over-browning.

Evaporated Cane Juice

Evaporated cane products are a healthier alternative to regular table sugar. They do undergo some processing but not to the same level as highly refined white sugar so they retain more vitamins and minerals. To make evaporated cane sugar, sugar cane is crushed and the juice crystals are washed, boiled, filtered, and dried. This process removes all of the plant material. It is available in a variety of textures and tastes, from coarse to fine, and from a distinctive to a subtle molasses flavor. Please note that it is still sugar and should be used in limited amounts, but it is a good choice when a dry sweetener is needed. Sucanat is minimally processed and has a rich molasses flavor, which makes it a good substitute for brown sugar.

Stevia to the Rescue

Stevia rebaudiana is a small green plant native to Paraguay that currently grows in parts of South America and Asia. It was used by early people in a tea-like beverage as well as for medicinal purposes. Today, stevia is commonly used in several parts of the world including South America, China, and Japan. Its leaves have a delicious taste that can be up to 30 times sweeter than sugar. Quality stevia leaves and whole leaf concentrate are natural and nutritious dietary supplements that offer numerous health benefits.

Processed stevia can be 200-300 times sweeter than sugar. In its pure, unadulterated form, it is safe for diabetics and does not adversely affect blood sugar. The sweet glycosides of the plant pass right through the body and are not metabolized, so the body does not obtain any calories from stevia. There can be a bitter component to the leaf, most intense in poor quality leaves. In good quality products the bitterness of the whole leaf product disappears. When it is properly diluted for consumption, it is excellent for baking and cooking because the glycosides do not break down with heat.

Most baked goods recipes work best when stevia is combined with some other sweetener. The baked goods recipes in Naturally Nutritious were written with an option to use just sugar, or a sugar and stevia combination. Results in taste and texture will differ slightly depending on which option you choose. When replacing sugar with stevia in an existing recipe, or choosing the sugar and stevia combination in this book, note that you might also have to slightly alter the amount of other ingredients because it is such a concentrated sweetener---if the batter is too thick, thin it a little with a few tablespoons of milk or agave nectar.

Although its popularity is growing, stevia is far less prevalent in the United States. However, now that it has been approved for sale in the U.S.A, it will be much more widely available in everyday products. Be careful about the stevia you choose. Buy organic stevia products that use a clean, pure water extraction process. Some companies process stevia with petrochemicals which are dangerous to your health. Quality varies among different stevia manufacturers. An inferior product will often have a bitter aftertaste.

Substituting stevia for sugar in recipes can be tricky. It is difficult to give an exact equivalent. Sour foods like cranberries and rhubarb need more sweetener than naturally sweet foods, some people prefer their food sweeter than others, and the quality, flavor, and sweetness differs greatly with different companies. I encourage you to try several different brands to see which you like best.

My favorite brands of stevia are Nutrition for Optimal Wellness (NOW) Foods, Steviva, and SweetLeaf. NOW Foods offers a variety of powdered and liquid forms of stevia---the Stevia Glycerite is my favorite. Steviva Brand carries powdered stevia extract and great tasting, easy to use powdered stevia blends. Their blends are great for baking, and mix well with liquids. Sweetleaf carries several different types and flavors of stevia. I use their liquid extract (Stevia Clear) to sweeten drinks and occasionally I add the powdered extract (Stevia Plus) to dry products when baking. Sweet Leaf has delicious flavored liquid extracts such as Dark Chocolate, Lemon Drop, English Toffee, Orange Valencia, and several others. They also have a convenient, portable 6 mL travel size that I carry with me. The recipes in Naturally Nutritious were written using Stevia Glycerite. It has a thick, syrupy consistency, great flavor, is easy to measure, and mixes well with liquids. Feel free to substitute any quality stevia product that you choose---just use the chart below for the equivalent amount. The NOW brand is available online, and in Vitamin Cottage Stores, Steviva is available online, and SweetLeaf is available online, at Whole Food Markets, and Vitamin Cottage Stores. To find out more about NOW Foods, Steviva, and SweetLeaf, please refer to the Resources section of this book.

Below is an approximate equivalency chart for different forms of stevia as compared to sugar.

Sugar Amount	Equiv. of Stevia Powdered Extract	Equiv. of Stevia Liquid Conc.	Equiv. of Stevia Glycerite
1 cup	1 teaspoon	1 teaspoon	1 teaspoon
1/2 cup	1/2 teaspoon	1/2 teaspoon	1/2 teaspoon
1/4 cup	1/4 teaspoon	1/4 teaspoon	1/4 teaspoon
1 tablespoon	1/8-1/4 teaspoon	6-10 drops	6-10 drops
1 teaspoon	1/16-1/8 tsp.	3-5 drops	3-5 drops

PANTRY LIST

Some people are into clothes, some are into shoes, and some are into cars. I am into food. I love to cook, try different recipes, and create my own new recipes. I even like to go to the health food store, walk up and down the aisles, look for new items, read the ingredient lists, and decide which new items I'd like to try.

We live in a world of convenience. I understand that it seems much easier to eat out, or order in, than to make meals from scratch every night. However, with a little preparation your family can enjoy homemade meals with little effort. Several of the recipes in this book can be prepared fully, or partially, and then frozen. Spend a few hours every couple of weeks to prepare and cook foods. Freeze soups, grilled meats, or a purchased precooked rotisserie chicken, then thaw and serve with a salad or add to soup. Chop salad vegetables and cook whole grain pasta and store in the fridge to make healthy, hearty salad prep a snap! Cut back on dining out and processed foods and eat home-made food more often. Your family's health is worth it!

I keep a stocked pantry to make meal preparation convenient and easy. With these items handy, all I have to do is pick up fresh ingredients to be able to make most recipes.

The following is a list of healthy items that I use on a regular basis and store in the pantry:

- coconut oil and unsweetened shredded coconut
- coconut milk (freeze remaining coconut milk in ice cube trays and thaw as needed, 1 cube=2 tablespoons)
- stevia glycerite
- evaporated cane sugar and organic brown sugar
- baking powder and baking soda
- vanilla extract
- agave nectar and honey(preferable raw)
- brown rice syrup
- dried fruits (dates, raisins, cranberries, cherries)
- organic chocolate and peanut butter chips
- quick oats and rolled oats
- unsweetened cocoa powder
- whole grains (brown rice, wild rice, quinoa)
- sea salt
- cooking spray
- a variety of vinegars (balsamic, apple cider, rice and white wine vinegars)
- a variety of canned beans (garbanzo beans, black beans, pinto beans)
- dried lentils
- natural/traditionally brewed soy sauce
- no MSG seasoning salt
- canned tomatoes and tomato sauce
- whole grain pasta (whole wheat, Kamut, brown rice)
- natural thickeners (arrowroot, xanthan gum, and non-GMO cornstarch)
- spices: ground cumin, black pepper, ground cinnamon, basil, oregano, mint, Italian seasoning, paprika, chile powder, ground ginger, dried mustard, thyme.
- almond milk (sold in asceptic containers)
- organic powdered milk and powdered buttermilk

Store the following items in the refrigerator or freezer to retain nutrients:

- sprouted grain breads and tortillas
- unsweetened applesauce
- plain low-fat yogurt
- maple syrup

- flours (whole wheat pastry flour, stone-ground whole wheat flour, unbleached all purpose/white flour. These keep fresh longer in the fridge)
- extra virgin olive oil (it will solidify when cold so let it sit at room temperature for a few minutes or run under warm water before using)
- grapeseed oil (can also be stored in a cool dark place)
- raw nuts and seeds(almonds, pine nuts, walnuts, pumpkin seeds, sunflower seeds)
- toasted wheat germ
- flaxseed meal (flaxseeds turn rancid quickly after they are ground. To get the most benefit from flaxseeds, grind them in a coffee grinder just before using)
- organic butter
- minced garlic
- lemon juice
- tomato paste (available in tubes--this makes it easy if I am only using a tablespoon at a time)

MILK CHOICES

When using milk in a recipe, choose from almond milk, coconut milk, rice milk, or organic cow's milk. Organic soymilk works well in recipes if you eat soy products. Although I am not a proponent of processed soy products, I do use plain soymilk in some recipes when I need a creamy milk with neutral flavor. Many people do not tolerate cow's milk well and the result is digestive problems. Milk is highly processed through pasteurization. This process destroys good bacteria, live enzymes, and vitamins. Conventional milk also contains antibiotics and growth hormones fed to cows. The least processed dairy products are the healthier choices. Although it can be difficult to find in the United States, raw milk is a great option. Raw milk and raw-milk cheeses are non-pasteurized and non-homogenized. They retain a variety of enzymes and are much easier to digest than pasteurized products. Try substitutes for dairy in your diet and you might be surprised at how delicious they are and how easy it is to incorporate them into foods.

ORGANIC FOODS

When possible, choose organic products, especially meat and dairy. I highly encourage eating a variety of fruits and vegetables even if organic produce is not available. The fruits and vegetables highest in pesticides are peaches, apples, nectarines, strawberries, cherries, grapes, pears, bell peppers, celery, lettuce, spinach and potatoes. Wash organic and conventional produce well with a purchased produce wash, or a vinegar and hydrogen peroxide method. For the vinegar method, you will need two spray bottles. Fill one with white vinegar and the other with 3 percent hydrogen peroxide (the same kind as in the drugstore). Spray fruits and vegetables first with vinegar then with peroxide, and rinse well. This method can also be used to sanitize counter tops.

If I am not able to buy organic, due to price or availability, I at least make sure to avoid synthetic, highly processed foods containing MSG, artificial flavors and colors, high-fructose corn syrup, preservatives, and hydrogenated fats. Eating foods as close to their natural state as possible is highly beneficial for you. Our bodies are not able to use artificial foods and they will actually damage your health. Eating processed foods over a period of years will make your body toxic, decrease your immune system, increase your weight, and impair your overall health.

For years, my motto has been "If you can't read it, don't eat it." In other words, if it is difficult to pronounce an ingredient on the label, your body won't be able to process it and it is usually not good for you. Read food labels. If a product contains any of the artificial elements mentioned above , do not buy it, do not keep it in your house, and do not eat it. Artificial ingredients are harmful to your health. Eliminate the foods that damage your body and replace them with a few healthy choices and it will benefit your health and can change your life.

Remember, this is not a diet. Instead, view these changes as steps toward a healthier you. Making all of the changes at once may seem overwhelming but please take it one step, or one recipe, at a time. Any healthy change is progress. Implement the following steps at your pace:

1) Remove processed, damaging foods from your kitchen. Eliminate foods containing hydrogenated or partially hydrogenated fat, MSG (also listed as anything "auto-lyzed" or "hydrolyzed"), processed foods, high-fructose corn syrup, preservatives, and bleached white flour as well as artificial sweeteners, colors, and flavors. Read food labels and eliminate anything with these ingredients. If these items are not in your house, you will be less likely to eat them. This easy step will make a noticeable improvement in your health.
2) Incorporate foods from the "pantry list" into your diet.
3) Experiment with your own recipes to replace the unhealthy ingredients with healthy choices. Try new recipes and introduce new foods to your family.

The recipes in this cookbook were created and tested in Denver. In Colorado, high altitude rules apply. If you don't live above 5000 feet, you may need to do one or more of the following for the baked goods to turn out well:

- Increase the amount of baking powder or baking soda.
- Decrease the oven temperature by 20 degrees.
- Decrease the amount of liquid by 2-3 tablespoons per cup of flour called for in the recipe
- Baking and cooking times may need to be adjusted

Please note that in the recipes in this book, 1-1/2 cups or 1-1/2 tablespoons means one and a half, not one to one half.

APPETIZERS AND SNACKS

CHAPTER TWO

Hummus

Feta and Parsley Hummus

Creamy Vegetable Dip

Eggplant Dip

Goat Cheese and Date Spread

Cold Spinach Dip

Creamy Spinach and Artichoke Dip

Guacamole

Green Pea Guacamole

Spiced Baked Tortilla Chips

Parmesan Pita Chips

Raw Spiced Almonds

Sweet Spiced Nuts

Maple Pecans

Layered Bean Dip

Spiced Honey Snack Mix

Honey Mustard Pretzels

Veggie Quesadillas

Stuffed Mushrooms

Edamame and Avocado Wontons

Spinach and Cheese Wonton Ravioli

HUMMUS

This dip is delicious, nutritious, and simple to make. There is no need to buy it—make your own at home. My oldest son loves to have his own bowl of hummus and whole grain crackers for lunch.

1 (15-ounce) can chickpeas (garbanzo beans), lightly drained
2 tablespoons tahini
1-1/2 tablespoons lemon juice
1 teaspoon minced garlic
1/4 teaspoon ground cumin
1/4 teaspoon salt
Dash black pepper
1/2 teaspoon agave nectar or honey
Dash nutmeg
2 tablespoons extra virgin olive oil or plain low-fat yogurt

In a food processor, pulse beans to chop. Add the tahini, lemon juice, garlic, cumin, salt, pepper, agave and nutmeg then pulse to mix. With the machine running, drizzle the olive oil and process until the mixture is smooth. If it is too thick, add one tablespoon of water. Adjust seasonings to your liking. Transfer to a dish and refrigerate until ready to serve.

Serve with raw vegetables, whole grain crackers, or tortilla chips.

Yield: 2 cups

For **Sun-dried Tomato Hummus**: Place 1/4 cup sun-dried tomatoes in a bowl and pour enough hot water over to completely cover. Let sit for 5 minutes then drain. Eliminate the nutmeg from the recipe. Add the sun-dried tomatoes to the hummus after adding the olive oil; pulse to chop or blend well to distribute the tomatoes evenly.

FETA AND PARSLEY HUMMUS

I love the combination of feta and hummus together. One of my favorite lunches is a chicken wrap with veggies, hummus and feta. This dip can be served hot or cold. To serve warm, place the dip in an oven-safe dish and set in a preheated 350 degree oven for 10 minutes or until heated through.

2 cups Hummus (see recipe above)
1 tablespoon dried parsley or 3 tablespoons chopped fresh parsley
1/2 cup crumbled feta cheese

Mix prepared hummus and parsley together in a bowl. Gently stir in feta cheese. Serve with whole grain crackers, raw vegetables, or Spiced Baked Tortilla Chips (see index).

Yield: 2-1/2 cups

CREAMY VEGETABLE DIP

Serve this dip with raw vegetables or organic potato chips. To prepare this dip really quickly, simply mix yogurt and sour cream with 2 tablespoons pre-made Nic's Mix (see index) and 2 teaspoons evaporated cane sugar or a few drops of stevia. If you are using onion salt and celery salt instead of powder, you may need to decrease the amount of salt. To turn this dip into salad dressing, simply thin it with a little milk, and vinegar or lemon juice.

3/4 cup plain low-fat yogurt
3/4 low-fat sour cream
1/2 teaspoon garlic powder
1 teaspoon salt
1/2 teaspoon onion powder or onion salt
1 teaspoon dried parsley
1/4 teaspoon celery seed or celery salt
1/8 teaspoon black pepper
2 teaspoons evaporated cane sugar or a few drops of stevia glycerite
1 tablespoon powdered milk (optional)

Mix all of the ingredients together in a small bowl and refrigerate for at least an hour before serving. Taste and adjust the seasonings to your liking. Cover and store in the fridge for up to a week.

Yield: 3/4 cup

TIP: For a thicker dip, replace the plain low-fat yogurt with yogurt cheese (see index) or Greek style yogurt(see glossary).

EGGPLANT DIP

1 medium eggplant
Olive oil
Salt and pepper
2 cloves garlic, minced (about 2 teaspoons)
3 tablespoons tahini
2 tablespoons plain yogurt
1/2 teaspoon salt
2 teaspoons lemon juice
Dash hot sauce
1 teaspoon dried parsley
1 teaspoon dried mint

Preheat oven to 350 degrees.

Cut the eggplant in half lengthwise, brush the flat sides with olive oil, and sprinkle with salt and pepper. Place the eggplant cut side down in an oven-safe dish and bake for 15-20 minutes or until it can be easily pierced with a fork.

Remove from the oven, place in a colander over a bowl to drain, let sit for 5 minutes, then discard the liquid. Scoop out the eggplant flesh and discard skin. Place the eggplant, garlic, tahini, yogurt, salt, lemon juice and hot sauce in a food processor and blend for 30 seconds. Add the parsley and mint and process for 15 seconds to incorporate herbs. Add salt and hot sauce to taste, then pour into a dish, cover, and refrigerate.

Serve with Spiced Baked Tortilla Chips or Parmesan Pita Chips (see index).

For Smoky Eggplant Dip: Add 1/2 teaspoon cumin and 1/2 teaspoon smoked paprika to dip before adding herbs.

TIP: Choose small to medium eggplants that feel plump, firm and heavy for their size. Larger eggplants tend to be more bitter.

GOAT CHEESE AND DATE SPREAD

This slightly sweet and tangy spread is delicious on crackers or slices of whole grain baguette.

3 tablespoons goat cheese
1/4 cup reduced-fat cream cheese
3 large dates, stems and pits removed, finely chopped
Chopped or sliced almonds for garnish

Mix the goat cheese and cream cheese in a bowl until creamy. Stir in the dates, transfer to a serving dish, and top with almonds.

Yield: 1/2 cup

COLD SPINACH DIP

1/4 cup cream cheese (low-fat or regular)
1/2 cup mayonnaise (low-fat or regular)
1/2 cup sour cream (low-fat or regular)
1 (10-ounce) package organic frozen spinach, thawed and drained
2 green onions, sliced into 1/2-inch pieces
1/2 teaspoon seasoning salt or Nic's Mix (see index)
1/8 teaspoon black pepper
1 teaspoon lemon juice
1/2 cup feta cheese, crumbled

In a large bowl, mix the cream cheese with a whisk until smooth. Mix in the mayonnaise and sour cream then add the spinach, onions, seasoning salt, pepper and lemon juice. Mix well, then gently stir in the feta cheese. Adjust seasonings to taste then refrigerate for at least an hour before serving.

Serve with Spiced Baked Tortilla Chips (see index), crackers, or fresh veggies.

Yield: 2-1/2 cups

CREAMY SPINACH AND ARTICHOKE DIP

This warm, creamy spinach dip is great for parties. It solidifies quickly, so transfer some to a serving bowl, and keep the rest warm on the stove or in a crockpot.

1 tablespoon coconut oil or extra virgin olive oi.
1/2 cup diced onion (about 1/2 medium)
1-1/2 tablespoons minced garlic (4-5 cloves)
1/2 cup unbleached all purpose flour
1-1/4 cups chicken broth
1 cup milk
3/4 cup freshly grated Parmesan cheese
2 tablespoons dry chicken bouillon
1-1/2 tablespoons fresh lemon juice
1 teaspoon evaporated cane sugar
1/4 teaspoon salt
1/8 teaspoon fresh ground black pepper
3/4 cup low-fat sour cream
1/2 (8-ounce) package low-fat cream cheese
12-ounces frozen spinach, thawed and drained
1 green onion, chopped into 1/2-inch pieces
1 cup canned artichokes, drained and chopped
1/2 teaspoon hot sauce
3/4 cup shredded Monterey Jack cheese or mozzarella cheese

In a large skillet, warm the coconut oil on medium-low heat. Add the diced onion and cook for 3-4 minutes then stir in the garlic and cook a few more minutes. Sprinkle the flour over the onions, stir and cook for 10 minutes. While stirring, slowly pour in the chicken broth. When the mixture begins to bubble, stir in the milk, then return to a simmer. Remove from the heat, add the Parmesan, dry chicken bouillon, lemon juice, sugar, salt and pepper. Add the sour cream, cream cheese, spinach, green onion, artichokes, hot sauce, and cheese. Stir until the cheese has melted then transfer to a serving dish. Serve warm.

Serve with Spiced Baked Tortilla Chips(see index), crackers, or whole grain bread.

Yield: 6 cups

CREAMY GUACAMOLE

1 large tomato (about 1 cup)
2 medium avocados
1/4 cup finely diced red onion
1 tablespoon fresh squeezed lime juice (about 1/2 small lime)
2 tablespoons chopped fresh cilantro
1 clove garlic, minced or 1 teaspoon garlic salt
1 teaspoon cumin
1/2 teaspoon salt
Dash hot sauce
2 tablespoons plain low-fat yogurt

Cut the top off the tomato, hold cut side down and gently squeeze out the excess liquid. Chop the tomato into 1/2-inch pieces and set aside. Cube the avocados and scoop the pulp into a medium bowl. Save one avocado pit for later. With a fork, mash the avocado but leave a chunky texture. Add the remaining ingredients and stir, then gently stir in the diced tomato. Place the avocado pit on top of the mixture and seal with plastic wrap, gently pushing the wrap directly onto the mixture to prevent the dip from browning.

Yield: 2-1/2 cups

GREEN PEA GUACAMOLE

This is a lighter but still tasty version of guacamole.

1/2 cup frozen peas, thawed
1/2 cup frozen or fresh broccoli (steamed until fork-tender)
2 garlic cloves, coarsely chopped
1/2 cup cottage cheese
1 teaspoon ground cumin
2 tablespoons fresh lime juice
1 teaspoon salt
2 tablespoons chopped fresh cilantro
1/2 teaspoon hot sauce
2 tomatoes, diced
1/4 cup red onion, diced
1 avocado, cubed (save the pit)

In a food processor, pulse the peas, broccoli, and garlic cloves to chop. Add the cottage cheese and puree until smooth. Transfer the mixture to a medium bowl. Stir in the cumin, lime juice, salt, cilantro, and hot sauce. Cut the tops off the tomatoes and squeeze gently over a sink or bowl to reduce excess liquid. Chop the tomatoes then add to pea mixture. Gently stir in the red onion and avocado. Place the avocado pit on top of the mixture and seal with plastic wrap, pushing the wrap directly onto the dip to prevent the dip from browning.

Yield: 2-1/2 cups

TIP: To cut an avocado, run a knife along the outside edge lengthwise. Twist both sides in opposite directions and separate. Set the side containing the pit on a flat surface. Tap the pit with a large knife and twist to pull it out. Run a paring knife along the length and width of the avocado to create cubes. Scoop out the pulp with a small spoon.

SPICED BAKED TORTILLA CHIPS

This is a simple, healthy chip to dip in salsa or hummus. The spice and sugar mixture can be replaced with 2 tablespoons Nic's Mix plus 1/4 teaspoon evaporated cane sugar. After the chips have been lightly seasoned, save the remaining mixture in an airtight container and use as a seasoning salt for meats, chips or vegetables.

1 (12-ounce) package sprouted grain tortillas, corn tortillas, or whole wheat tortillas
Cooking spray
1 teaspoon garlic salt or garlic powder
1-1/2 teaspoons salt
1 teaspoon onion powder
1/2 teaspoon paprika
1/2 teaspoon chili powder
1/2 teaspoon evaporated cane sugar

Preheat the oven to 375 degrees.

Mix the garlic salt, salt, onion powder, paprika, chili powder, and sugar in a small bowl and set aside. Cut the tortillas into wedges, or 2-inch pieces, and place in a large bowl. Spray with oil then sprinkle with some of the spice mixture; stir to coat. Repeat until the tortilla pieces are lightly seasoned. Arrange the pieces in a single layer on a baking sheet. Bake on the center rack for 10 minutes or until the chips are lightly browned and crisp; flip chips after 5 minutes to brown evenly. Remove from the oven, let the chips cool on the pan for 10 minutes then transfer to an airtight container. Repeat with the remaining tortilla pieces.

<u>Variation:</u> Brush tortillas with peanut oil or grapeseed oil, cut tortillas into 2-inch pieces, place in a single layer on a cookie sheet, sprinkle with spices and bake as instructed above.

For <u>Baked Tortilla Chips:</u> Spray a cookie sheet with cooking spray. Arrange sprouted grain, whole wheat or corn tortilla pieces in a single layer on a pan. Coat pieces with cooking spray then grind coarse salt onto each chip. Bake on the center rack in a preheated 375 degree oven for 10 minutes or until the chips are lightly browned and crisp; flip chips after 5 minutes. Remove from the oven, let the chips cool on the pan for 10 minutes then transfer to an airtight container. Repeat with the remaining tortillas pieces.

PARMESAN PITA CHIPS

4 sprouted wheat or whole wheat pita breads
1/2 teaspoon garlic salt
1/2 teaspoon salt
1/4 teaspoon evaporated cane sugar
2–3 tablespoons grated or shredded Parmesan cheese
Cooking spray

Preheat the oven to 350 degrees.

Cut the pitas into wedges, or 2-inch pieces, and place in a bowl. Mix the garlic salt, salt, and sugar in a small bowl. Spray pita pieces lightly with oil, then sprinkle with half of the seasoning mixture. Stir, then repeat with oil and remaining seasoning. Arrange the pieces in a single layer on a sprayed cookie sheet. Bake on the center rack for 10 minutes, remove from the oven and sprinkle with Parmesan cheese. Bake for a few more minutes or until the cheese is melted and the chips are crisp and lightly browned. Remove from the oven and let cool completely. Store in an airtight container.

For Garlic Pita Chips: Eliminate the Parmesan cheese. Sprinkle 1 tablespoon of minced garlic on top of pita pieces and bake for 10-15 minutes or until chips are crispy and lightly browned.

RAW SPICED ALMONDS

These nuts are cooked on low heat for just a few minutes to retain maximum nutrients. They are a superbly healthy snack. If you don't like the chewy texture of raw nuts, follow the cooking instructions below for Spiced Almonds.

2 teaspoons coconut oil
3 cups raw almonds
1 teaspoon garlic salt
1/2 teaspoon onion salt
1 teaspoon chili powder
1/2 teaspoon cinnamon
1/2 teaspoon salt
Dash ground mustard
Dash cayenne pepper
2 tablespoons evaporated cane sugar

Mix the garlic salt, onion salt, chili powder, cinnamon, salt, mustard, cayenne, and sugar in a small bowl and set aside. In a large frying pan, melt oil on low heat. Pour almonds into the pan and toss to coat. Sprinkle with seasoning mixture and stir to coat completely. Remove from the heat and spread onto wax paper to cool. Store in the fridge in an airtight container.

Yield: 3 cups

For <u>Spiced Almonds:</u> Preheat oven to 300 degrees. After coating nuts with seasonings, spread them on a greased baking sheet. Bake for 15 minutes, flip them over then bake for another 15 minutes. Remove from the oven and let cool completely. Store in an airtight container.

For <u>Cocoa Spiced Almonds:</u> Add 2 tablespoons unsweetened cocoa powder and 1/4 cup evaporated cane sugar to the seasoning mixture and follow directions for Spiced Almonds.

TIP: Nuts spoil easily due to their high oil content. Store them in the fridge to retain the nutrients, enzymes, and beneficial fats. Heating raw nuts reduces their omega-3 content.

SWEET SPICED NUTS

4 cups mixed raw nuts (your choice of raw walnuts, almonds, pecans, pumpkin
seeds etc...)
2 teaspoons ground cinnamon
1/2 teaspoon ground cumin
1/2 teaspoon ground ginger
1/4 teaspoon ground cloves
1/4 teaspoon ground nutmeg
1 teaspoon chili powder
1–1/4 teaspoons salt
1/4 cup maple syrup
1/4 cup brown sugar

Preheat oven to 300 degrees. Spray a large baking sheet with cooking spray.

Mix the cinnamon, cumin, ginger, cloves, nutmeg, chili powder, and salt in a small bowl
and set aside. In a large frying pan stir the maple syrup and brown sugar on low heat
until the sugar dissolves. Stir in the seasoning mixture until well incorporated. Add nuts
and stir to coat completely. Pour onto the prepared pan and bake for 40 minutes, stirring
every 10 minutes. Remove from the oven and spread onto wax paper to cool. Break into
small pieces and store in an airtight container.

Yield: 4 cups

TIP: Almonds are a good source of calcium and Vitamin E and are beneficial for the
gastrointestinal tract.

MAPLE PECANS/WALNUTS

These nuts are great as a snack or sprinkled onto Blue Cheese and Walnut Salad(see index).

2 teaspoons coconut oil
1/4 cup maple syrup
2 tablespoons brown sugar
1/4 teaspoon salt
1/4 teaspoon cinnamon
2 cups raw pecans or walnuts

In a large frying pan, melt the coconut oil on low heat. Add the maple syrup, brown sugar, salt, and cinnamon; stir until the sugar dissolves. Add nuts and toss to coat thoroughly. Remove from the heat and pour onto wax paper in a single layer to cool. Store in the fridge in an airtight container.

Yield: 2 cups

TIP: *Walnuts are high in omega-3 fatty acids which decrease inflammation and can prevent heart disease.*

LAYERED BEAN DIP

This dip tastes even better the next day. If you don't have guacamole prepared, mash 2 avocados and stir them into the sour cream mixture.

1 (15-ounce) can refried beans
1/4 teaspoon ground cumin
1/4 teaspoon garlic salt
1 cup sour cream (low-fat or regular)
2 tablespoons chopped fresh cilantro
1 teaspoon lime juice
1 cup salsa
1/2 cup corn niblets
1 cup prepared guacamole
1 cup shredded cheddar or Monterey Jack cheese
1 cup chopped lettuce
1 cup chopped tomato
1 tablespoon finely diced jalapeno pepper (optional)
2 green onions, sliced into 1/2-inch pieces

Empty the can of refried beans into a bowl and stir in the cumin and garlic salt. In a separate bowl, mix the sour cream with cilantro and lime juice. Mix the tomato with the jalapeno and green onions in a third bowl. Spread the beans onto a platter. Spread the sour cream on top, then layer the salsa, corn, and guacamole. Sprinkle with cheese, lettuce, and tomato mixture. Refrigerate to cool.

Serve with tortilla chips.

SPICED HONEY SNACK MIX

This mix is easy to make and even easier to snack on. It is good any time of the year but I tend to make it around Thanksgiving to set out for guests.

1 cup O's cereal.
2 cups rice or corn squares cereal
2 cups wheat squares cereal
3 cups pretzels
1 cup mixed nuts
1 cup cheddar bunny crackers
4 tablespoons butter
5 tablespoons agave nectar or honey
1 teaspoon seasoning salt
1/4 teaspoon celery salt
1 teaspoon garlic powder
1 teaspoon onion salt
3/4 teaspoon chili powder
1-1/2 tablespoons Worcestershire sauce

Preheat oven to 250 degrees.

Mix cereals, pretzels, nuts, and crackers in a large bowl. Melt the butter in a small saucepan. Stir in the agave nectar, seasonings, and Worcestershire sauce. Pour half of the butter mixture over the dry ingredients and stir. Add the rest of the butter and stir well to coat. Spread the snack mixture onto a greased cookie sheet. Bake for 1 hour, stirring every 15 minutes. Remove from the oven and let cool, then transfer to an airtight container. Store in an airtight container for up to 2 weeks.

Yield: 10 cups

HONEY MUSTARD PRETZELS

1/4 cup butter
1/4 cup agave nectar or honey
1/4 cup prepared yellow mustard
1 tablespoon Worcestershire sauce
1/2 teaspoon salt
1/4 teaspoon onion salt
1/8 teaspoon ground ginger
Dash hot sauce
10 cups pretzels
Extra salt for sprinkling

Preheat oven to 300 degrees.

Melt the butter in a saucepan over low heat. Remove from the heat and stir in agave, mustard, Worcestershire, salt, onion salt, ginger, and hot sauce. Place the pretzels in a large bowl, pour the agave mixture on top and stir to coat evenly. Arrange the pretzels on a greased cookie sheet. Bake for 25 minutes, stirring every 10 minutes. Remove from the oven and sprinkle with salt while still warm. Pour the pretzels onto wax paper to cool. Store in an airtight container.

Yield: 10 cups

GRANOLA SNACK MIX

This mix is great for an on-the-go snack or to set out at parties. This version is slightly sticky and chewy. If you prefer it crunchier, increase baking time to 30-35 minutes.

1/3 cup apricot or apple jelly (fruit juice sweetened)
2 tablespoons brown sugar or evaporated cane sugar
6 tablespoons brown rice syrup, agave nectar or honey (or a mixture)
1 tablespoon coconut oil or butter
1/2 teaspoon cinnamon
1/8 teaspoon salt
2 tablespoons unsweetened shredded coconut (optional)
1-3/4 cup rolled oats
1/2 coarsely chopped or sliced raw almonds
1/4 cup raw sunflower seeds or pumpkin seeds
3/4 cup raisins
1/2 cup broken pretzels
1/2 cup chocolate chips

Preheat oven to 325 degrees.

In a small saucepan, measure the jelly, brown sugar, brown rice syrup, coconut oil, and cinnamon. Cook and stir over low heat until the sugar dissolves. Remove from the heat and stir in the salt and shredded coconut.

Mix the oats, nuts, and seeds in a large bowl. Pour the liquid mixture on top and stir well to coat. The mixture should look wet; add more agave if needed. Pour onto a greased baking sheet and spread into an even layer. Bake for 20-25 minutes or until lightly browned. Stir 2-3 times while baking.

Remove from the oven and stir in the raisins and pretzels. Transfer the mixture to a piece of wax paper or aluminum foil to cool, then stir in chocolate chips. Store in an airtight container for up to two weeks.

-

VEGGIE QUESADILLAS

Each quesadilla can be cut into 4 pieces and served as an appetizer, or the entire quesadilla can be served as a meal.

4 (10-inch) sprouted grain or whole wheat tortillas
2 teaspoons olive oil or coconut oil
1/2 medium red onion, diced (about 1/2 cup)
1/2 green pepper, diced
1/2 red bell pepper, diced
1/2 cup zucchini, diced
1 teaspoon cumin
1/2 teaspoon garlic salt
1/2 teaspoon dried oregano
1/2 cup goat cheese, crumbled
1 cup shredded mozzarella
1/2 cup Monterey Jack or cheddar cheese
Sour cream, sliced avocado, salsa for garnish

In a large frying pan, heat the oil on medium heat. Cook and stir the onion for a few minutes then add the green pepper, red bell pepper, zucchini, cumin, garlic salt and oregano. Continue to cook for 5 minutes or until the veggies are fork-tender then transfer to a bowl.

In the same pan, on medium heat, place a tortilla. Spread 1/4 cup mozzarella, half of the goat cheese and half of the Monterey Jack onto the tortilla. Spread half of the veggies on top of the cheese then top with 1/4 cup mozzarella and another tortilla. Cook for 5 minutes or until the cheese is melted and the bottom tortilla is lightly browned. Carefully flip the quesadilla over and cook the other side for 5 minutes. Transfer to a plate and repeat with remaining tortillas and fillings.

Quesadillas can also be heated in the oven. To bake, assemble the quesadillas on a baking sheet instead of the pan. Cook in a preheated 350 degree oven for 10 min or until cheese is melted.

Cut each quesadilla into 4 pieces with a pizza cutter and top with a dollop of sour cream, a spoonful of salsa, and a few slices of avocado.

Yield: 16 pieces

STUFFED MUSHROOMS

12 large white button mushrooms
2 teaspoons olive oil
1/4 cup diced yellow onion
1 garlic clove, minced (about 1 teaspoon)
1/2 (10-ounce) package frozen spinach, thawed
1 teaspoon dried basil
1 teaspoon dried oregano
2 slices nitrate-free turkey bacon, cooked and diced
1/4 cup feta cheese, crumbled
1/4 cup dry whole wheat bread crumbs
1/4 teaspoon salt
1/8 teaspoon pepper
1/2 cup shredded mozzarella

Preheat oven to 350 degrees.

Clean mushrooms and remove stems. Place mushroom caps stem-side down on a greased baking dish and bake for 5 minutes. While the mushrooms are cooking, chop the mushroom stems. When the mushrooms are tender, remove the pan from the oven and set aside. Place the spinach in the middle of a clean dish towel and fold over the spinach. Twist ends in opposite directions to squeeze out water.

Heat oil in a medium frying pan and sauté the mushroom stems with the chopped onion and garlic until the onions are translucent, about 5 minutes. Add the spinach, basil, and oregano, and stir. Remove from the heat and transfer to a bowl. Stir the bacon, feta, bread crumbs, salt, and pepper into the spinach mixture.

Place mushrooms stem-side up on a greased baking dish. Scoop a tablespoon of the spinach mixture into each mushroom. Sprinkle with mozzarella and bake for 15 minutes or until the cheese is melted and golden brown.

Yield: 12 mushrooms

TIP: 1 medium onion equals approximately 1 to 1-1/4 cups diced onion, 1 large onion equals 1-1/2 to 2 cups diced onion.

SPINACH AND CHEESE WONTON RAVIOLI

These wontons can be boiled ravioli-style, fried, or baked, and served as an appetizer or side dish. Serve with warm pasta sauce for dipping.

Cooking spray or 1 teaspoon coconut oil
1 medium yellow onion, finely diced
2 garlic cloves, minced
2 (10-ounce) packages of frozen spinach, thawed and drained (about 2-1/2 cups)
2 teaspoons lemon juice
1/4 teaspoon ground nutmeg
3/4 teaspoon salt
1/4 teaspoon ground pepper
1 teaspoon dried basil
1/2 cup shredded mozzarella
1/4 cup shredded Parmesan cheese
32 wonton wrappers
Coconut oil or grapeseed oil for frying

In a large frying pan, melt the coconut oil on medium heat. Add the onion and garlic and cook for 5 minutes. Stir in the spinach, lemon juice, nutmeg, salt, pepper, and basil, and cook for a few more minutes until the onion is translucent. Remove from the heat and add the mozzarella and Parmesan. Stir thoroughly.

Fill a small bowl with water and set aside. Set out 6-8 wonton wrappers. Spoon 1 rounded teaspoon of the spinach mixture into the middle of each wrapper. Using a pastry brush, wet the outer half-inch of each wonton wrapper. Fold to form a triangle or rectangle and seal the edges with your fingers. Repeat with the remaining wrappers and filling.

To Boil: Bring salted water to a boil in a deep saucepan, add 4-6 wontons at a time, boil for 30 seconds, then transfer to a plate.

To Fry: Do not boil wontons. Measure 1 teaspoon oil into a medium(10-inch) nonstick frying pan and set on medium-high heat. Add 4-6 wontons and cook for 2 minutes. Flip wontons over and cook the other side for 60-90 seconds or until golden brown. Transfer to a plate, tent with foil, and repeat with the remaining wontons.

To Bake: Preheat oven to 450 degrees. Do not boil wontons. Place assembled wontons on a greased cookie sheet and spray generously with cooking spray. Bake for 5 minutes, flip, spray with cooking spray again, and bake for 2-3 minutes or until brown and crispy. Serve cooked wontons with warm pasta sauce.

Yield: 4-6 servings

For <u>Spinach Feta Wontons:</u> Eliminate Parmesan cheese and add 1/4 cup crumbled feta cheese

TIP: Cooked spinach is equal to one quarter of the amount of fresh (2 cups fresh spinach equals 1/2 cup cooked spinach).

EDAMAME AND AVOCADO WONTONS

Serve these delicious wontons with store bought Sweet Red Chili Sauce or Apricot Chili Garlic Sauce (see below). If you prefer a hotter flavor, add more wasabi powder. It takes very little oil to fry the wontons. If you are using a larger skillet, add 1-2 teaspoons more oil.

2 cups shelled edamame beans or green peas
3 tablespoons red onion or 2 green onions, diced
1 teaspoon minced garlic
2 teaspoons freshly grated ginger
4 teaspoons fresh lemon or lime juice
1–2 tablespoons wasabi powder
1 medium avocado
1/2 teaspoon salt
36–40 wonton wrappers
Coconut oil or grapeseed oil for frying

Measure the edamame, onions, garlic, ginger, and lemon juice into a food processor. Pulse until the edamame is chopped. Add the wasabi, avocado, and salt; turn the processor on and puree for 30 seconds or until the mixture is smooth.

Fill a small bowl with water. Set out 6 wonton wrappers out at a time. Spoon 1 rounded teaspoon of the filling into the middle of each wrapper. With a pastry brush, wet the outer half-inch of each wrapper. Fold one edge over the filling to form a triangle or rectangle. Press the edges to seal. Repeat with remaining wrappers and filling. Wontons can be baked or fried:

To fry: Measure 1 teaspoon of oil into a medium (10-inch) nonstick frying pan and set on medium-high heat. Add 6 wontons in a single layer and cook for 2 minutes, flip wontons, add 1 more teaspoon oil, and cook for another 60-90 seconds or until the wontons are browned. Transfer to a plate and tent with foil. Repeat with the remaining wontons.

To bake: Preheat oven to 450 degrees. Arrange the wontons on a greased cookie sheet and spray generously with cooking spray. Bake for 5 minutes, turn over, spray with cooking spray again, and bake other side for 2-3 minutes or until brown and crispy.

Yield: 6-8 servings

T CHILI GARLIC SAUCE

d apricot jam

auce

e vinegar

lic sauce and rice vinegar in a small bowl and use as a dipping

ns can be frozen for up to 1 month. To freeze, arrange wontons in
ting sheet. When frozen, transfer wontons to an airtight container
Remove as needed. Add an extra few minutes of cooking time when
ns.

Pasta Francine (Serves 4)

Rainbow Chard will keep its color when cooked

1. Tear Rainbow Chard into 2" pieces.
2. Add to boiling water with 1 cup of penne pasta.
3. Cook until pasta is al dente.
4. Drain and toss in olive oil and 1 tsp. chopped garlic.
5. Salt, pepper, parmesan, to taste.

"Malto bene!"

Lakeside Organic Gardens
Watsonville, CA 95076
Produce of U.S.A.

cooking,

BREADS AND PANCAKES

CHAPTER THREE

Zucchini Parmesan QuickBread

Honey Whole Grain Bread

Whole Grain Bagel Breadsticks

Whole Wheat Pizza Crust

Wheat Germ Pancakes

Oatmeal Raisin Pancakes

Whole Wheat French Toast

Whole Wheat Crepes with Peach Sauce

ZUCCHINI PARMESAN QUICKBREAD

This delicious bread pairs well with chili or Chicken Corn Chowder (see index). This recipe makes a big loaf. If you have leftovers, wrap portions in aluminum foil, place in a resealable plastic bag and freeze.

1 cup whole wheat pastry flour
1-1/2 cups unbleached all purpose flour
3 tablespoons evaporated cane sugar
1-1/2 tablespoons baking powder
1-1/2 teaspoons salt
1/8 teaspoon freshly ground black pepper
1/2 cup grated Parmesan or cheddar cheese
3 tablespoons butter
1/4 cup low-fat sour cream
1/4 cup diced yellow onion
1 cup shredded zucchini
3/4 cup milk
2 eggs
Grated Parmesan for topping

Preheat oven to 375 degrees. Spray a 9 by 5 inch loaf pan with cooking spray.

In a bowl, combine both flours, sugar, baking powder, salt, pepper, and Parmesan cheese. Place the zucchini in a separate bowl.

Melt the butter in a small saucepan then stir in the sour cream and onion. Add the butter mixture to the bowl with the zucchini, then stir in the milk and eggs. Combine the wet and dry ingredients and stir just until moistened. Pour into the prepared pan and bake for 15 minutes, remove from the oven and sprinkle the top with a few tablespoons of Parmesan cheese. Bake for 20-25 minutes more or until the top is golden brown and a toothpick comes out clean. Cool in the pan for 5 minutes on a wire rack then remove from pan.

Yield: 12-16 servings

TIP: If a piece of eggshell ends up in your batter, use half of the cracked eggshell to easily scoop it up.

HONEY WHOLE GRAIN BREAD

This delicious dense bread is high in fiber. It will fill you up and keep you satisfied. The apple cider vinegar adds great flavor and texture.

2 cups stone-ground whole wheat flour
1-1/2 teaspoons sea salt
1 cup unbleached bread flour or unbleached all purpose flour
1/4 cup semolina flour or dark rye flour
2 tablespoons honey or agave nectar
1 tablespoon barley malt or increase honey to 3 tablespoons
1 tablespoon apple cider vinegar
2 tablespoons raw sunflower seeds
1 tablespoon whole flax seeds
2 tablespoons raw pumpkin seeds
2-1/2 teaspoons active dry yeast
1-1/2 cups warm water

Bread Machine Method:

Measure the whole wheat flour, salt, bread flour, semolina flour, honey, barley malt, apple cider vinegar, seeds, and yeast into the bread machine pan. Pour warm water on top and set on dough cycle. When the cycle starts, check the dough for consistency. The dough should form a slightly sticky ball. If the dough is too dry, add a small amount of water, if it is too wet, add some flour.

Preheat the oven to 350 degrees. As soon as the cycle is done, remove dough and shape into 2 loaves or 12 buns. Set loaves on a greased baking sheet. Cover and let rise in a warm place for 30 minutes. Cut 3 diagonal slits on top of bread. Bake for 20-25 minutes or until golden brown and firm when touched.

Manual Method:

In a small bowl, dissolve yeast and honey in warm water and set aside. In a large bowl or bowl of electric mixer, combine all of the ingredients, stirring in yeast last. Knead dough by hand for about 10 minutes on a lightly floured surface or with a mixer for 5 minutes until smooth. Place dough in a well-greased bowl, turning the dough so the oil coats it. Cover the dough with a clean kitchen towel and set it in a warm place for 30 minutes. Preheat oven to 350 degrees. Shape dough into 2 loaves or 12 buns, cover with a towel again and let rest for another 30 minutes. Bake for 20-25 minutes or until golden brown.

Yield: 2 loaves, 10 slices each

TIPS:
- *For a chewy crust, spritz bread with water while baking, or fill an oven-safe dish halfway with water and place in oven while the bread is baking.*

• For a shiny crust mix one egg white with 1 tablespoon water and beat with a whisk. Brush the egg mixture onto the bread before baking.
• If the bread is browning too quickly, cover lightly with aluminum foil for the last 10 minutes of baking.

WHOLE GRAIN BAGEL BREADSTICKS

1 recipe Honey Whole Grain Bread
Water for boiling
1 egg white
1 tablespoon water

Measure the ingredients for the Honey Whole Grain Bread recipe into a bread machine pan and set on dough cycle. Remove the dough from the machine after 45 minutes. Preheat oven to 350 degrees. Fill a large pot with water and set on high heat to boil.

Set dough on a floured surface, divide into 8 pieces and roll into breadsticks. Place into boiling water, four at a time. Boil for 60 seconds, flipping after 30 seconds. Remove with a slotted spoon and place on a paper towel. Mix the egg white and water in a small bowl. Place breadsticks on a greased baking sheet and brush with egg wash. Bake for approximately 15 minutes or until light golden brown.

For **Bagels:** Form into bagel shape instead of breadsticks. Boil as instructed above, remove with a slotted spoon and place on a paper. Brush dough with egg wash, sprinkle with poppy seeds or sesame seeds, and set on a greased baking sheet. Bake for 20 minutes or until golden brown.

TIP: Barley malt gives the breadsticks or bagels that nice, chewy bagel consistency.

WHOLE WHEAT PIZZA CRUST

2 cups stone ground whole wheat flour
1-1/2 teaspoons sea salt
2 cups unbleached bread flour or unbleached all purpose flour
1 tablespoon honey or evaporated cane sugar
1 package (1/4-ounce) active dry yeast (2-1/4 teaspoons)
1-1/2 cups plus 1 tablespoon warm water
2 tablespoons extra virgin olive oil

Bread Machine Method:

Measure the whole wheat flour, salt, unbleached flour, honey, and yeast into the bread machine pan. Pour warm water on top and set machine on dough cycle. When the machine starts to mix, check the dough consistency. It should form a ball while kneading but should feel slightly sticky to the touch. Add more flour or water if needed. When the cycle is finished, remove dough from the pan and divide in half. Keeping one half covered, roll the other half into a 12-inch circle on a lightly floured surface. Transfer to a pizza pan and brush with olive oil. Repeat with second ball of dough. Add your favorite toppings and bake for 10-12 minutes in a preheated 450 degree oven.

Manual Method:

In a small bowl, dissolve yeast and honey in warm water and set aside. Combine the whole wheat flour, salt, and bread flour in a large bowl, stirring in yeast last. Knead by hand for five minutes or until the dough forms a ball. Turn the dough out onto a lightly floured surface and knead for about 30 seconds or until smooth. Place the dough into a well-oiled bowl and turn the dough so the oil coats it. Cover with a clean kitchen towel and set it in a warm place for about 1 hour to let the dough rise. When the dough has doubled in size, remove from the bowl and divide in half.

Keeping one half covered, roll out the other half into a 12-inch circle. Transfer to a pizza pan and brush with olive oil. Repeat with the second ball of dough. Add your favorite toppings and bake for 10-12 minutes in a preheated 450 degree oven.

Yield: 2 (12-inch) pizza crusts

TIP: When using a bread machine, do not add salt and yeast together. The salt will deactivate the yeast and the bread will not rise if the two ingredients are touching. To ensure that the yeast does not become deactivated. add the salt between flour additions and make sure the water is not too hot.

WHEAT GERM PANCAKES

These pancakes are high in fiber and low in fat.

1–1/2 cups whole wheat flour or whole wheat pastry flour
1/3 cup toasted wheat germ (or a mixture of wheat germ and flaxseed meal)
1 tablespoon baking powder
1/2 teaspoon salt
2–3 tablespoons brown sugar
1/2 teaspoon cinnamon
1 egg or 2 egg whites
2 tablespoons grapeseed oil or unsweetened applesauce
1–1/2 to 2 cups milk
Coconut oil or cooking spray

In a large bowl, mix the flour, wheat germ, baking powder, salt, brown sugar, and cinnamon. In a separate bowl mix the egg and oil. Stir in 1-1/2 cups milk, then add wet ingredients to dry. Stir just until moistened then adjust consistency by adding more milk or flour.

Melt 1 teaspoon of coconut oil in a skillet on medium-high heat. Drop batter onto the hot pan and cook for 60-90 seconds until bubbles form on top and the bottom is golden brown. Flip to cook the other side for 30-60 seconds then transfer to a plate. Repeat with remaining batter, adding oil as needed.

Yield: 18 pancakes

For <u>Banana Wheat Germ Pancakes</u> - Replace egg with 1 medium mashed banana. For <u>Blueberry Wheat Germ Pancakes</u> - After mixing wet and dry ingredients, gently stir in 1/2 cup frozen blueberries.

TIP: To freeze extra pancakes or french toast: arrange pieces in a single layer on a baking sheet and freeze. Transfer to a resealable plastic bag and store in the freezer. Take out as many as needed and thaw in a toaster or microwave.

OATMEAL RAISIN PANCAKES

These pancakes are thick and hearty. For an on-the-go snack, make a peanut butter and jam pancake sandwich!

1/2 cup unsweetened applesauce
1/2 cup plain yogurt
1 egg or 2 egg whites
1/4 cup brown sugar or maple syrup
1 teaspoon pure vanilla extract
1 cup quick oats
2 cups whole wheat pastry flour
1/2 cup raisins
1 tablespoon baking powder
1 teaspoon baking soda
1/2 teaspoon salt
2 teaspoons cinnamon
2 cups milk
Coconut oil or cooking spray

Whisk the applesauce, yogurt, egg, brown sugar, and vanilla in a large bowl. Add the oats, flour, raisins, baking powder, baking soda, salt, and cinnamon on top of the dry ingredients and stir to combine. Stir in 2 cups of milk just until combined. Do not over mix. Set the batter aside for 5 minutes then stir before using.

Spray a skillet with cooking spray or add 1 teaspoon of coconut oil to a skillet and set on medium-high heat. When the pan is hot, drop batter onto the pan to make 3 or 4 pancakes. Cook for 60-90 seconds or until the bottoms are golden brown. Turn to cook the other side for 30-60 seconds then transfer to a plate. Continue with remaining batter, adding oil if the pancakes begin to stick. The batter will thicken as it sits; add milk as needed.

Yield: 24 pancakes

TIP: Make sure the pan is hot before cooking pancake batter. The first few pancakes are often experimental and do not turn out well. They will cook more evenly as the pan comes to the right temperature. If the pancakes are browning too much on the bottom before the top is cooking, reduce the heat to medium.

WHOLE WHEAT FRENCH TOAST

8 slices whole wheat or sprouted grain bread, day–old or lightly toasted
3 eggs or 2 eggs and 2 egg whites
3 tablespoons milk
1 tablespoon brown sugar
1/2 teaspoon cinnamon
1/4 teaspoon salt
1 teaspoon pure vanilla extract
Cooking spray or coconut oil
Powdered sugar for sprinkling (optional)

Mix the eggs, milk, brown sugar, cinnamon, salt, and vanilla in a flat-bottomed dish. Coat a large skillet with cooking spray and set on medium-high heat. Place 1 slice of bread in the egg mixture, let soak for 30-60 seconds, then flip to saturate other side. Transfer to the preheated frying pan and cook for 3 minutes or until the bottom is golden brown. Turn to cook other side then transfer to a plate. Repeat with remaining bread slices.

When all the slices are cooked, sprinkle with powdered sugar. Top with fresh fruit and serve with maple syrup or sweetened yogurt.

Yield: 4 servings

For <u>French Toast Strips:</u> eliminate powdered sugar. Cut each slice of cooked french toast into 3 or 4 strips. Place strips in a freezer-safe container with space between each piece. Freeze in a single layer, then transfer to a resealable plastic bag. Remove as many strips as needed and reheat in a 350 degree oven for a few minutes or in a toaster or microwave. Serve strips with a side of maple syrup for dipping. These make a great breakfast treat for kids.

WHOLE WHEAT CREPES

These take a little time to make but are great for a special breakfast. To freeze, stack cooked crepes with a piece of wax paper between each and freeze flat. Take out as needed and reheat in a warm pan or in the microwave.

2 eggs
1 cup milk
2 teaspoons evaporated cane sugar
1 teaspoon pure vanilla extract
1 cup whole wheat pastry flour
1/4 teaspoon cinnamon (optional)
1/4 teaspoon salt
2 teaspoons coconut oil or butter, melted
3–4 tablespoons water

Measure the eggs, milk, sugar, and vanilla into a blender and mix on medium-high speed for a few seconds. Add flour, cinnamon, salt, oil, and water, then blend until smooth. Refrigerate batter for 30-60 minutes.

To cook crepes, lightly oil an 8-10 inch nonstick frying pan and set on medium-high heat. Pour about 2 tablespoons of crepe batter into the middle of the pan. Immediately lift pan to swirl batter to make a larger, really thin circle. Cook for 30-60 seconds then slide onto a plate. Do not flip. Roll crepe immediately or put a piece of wax paper in between each crepe to stack. Refrigerate for up to two days, or place in a resealable plastic bag and freeze for up to one month.

To serve, top with Peach Sauce (see below), sweetened yogurt and fresh fruit, or sauteed apples.

PEACH SAUCE

1 (15-ounce) can unsweetened peaches with juice, sliced
1 teaspoon vanilla
1/4 teaspoon liquid stevia glycerite or 1/4 cup brown sugar
1/4 cup orange juice
1 tablespoon arrowroot or cornstarch

In a medium saucepan, warm peaches, vanilla, and stevia on medium heat. Stir to mix. In a small bowl, mix orange juice with cornstarch, then add to peach mixture while stirring. Stir until thickened then transfer to a bowl, or spoon onto rolled crepes before serving. Top with a dollop of Sweet Yogurt Cream (see index).

MUFFINS AND LOAVES

CHAPTER FOUR

When using milk in baked goods, choose from almond milk, coconut milk, organic cow's milk, or rice milk. For the best baking results, bring eggs, applesauce and agave to room temperature before using. The thickness of the batter will differ slightly depending on whether sugar or stevia is used. The batter consistency may need to be adjusted with a few tablespoons of milk or flour.

PEACH MUFFINS

2 cups whole wheat pastry flour
1-1/2 teaspoons baking powder
1/2 teaspoon baking soda
3/4 teaspoon salt
1/2 teaspoon allspice
1 egg
1/2 cup plain low-fat yogurt
1/2 cup unsweetened applesauce
1/4 cup agave nectar or honey
1/4 cup brown sugar
1/2 teaspoon stevia glycerite or 1/2 cup evaporated cane sugar
1/3 cup milk
1 cup chopped peaches (canned, fresh or frozen and thawed)

Preheat oven to 350 degrees. Coat a 12-cup muffin pan with cooking spray.

Mix the flour, baking powder, baking soda, salt, and allspice in a large bowl. In a separate bowl, mix the egg, yogurt, applesauce, agave, brown sugar, and stevia. Whisk in milk, then gently stir in the peaches. Pour liquid mixture into dry and stir just until combined. Spoon batter into muffin tins and bake for 18-20 minutes or until a toothpick comes out clean. Let cool for 10 minutes then remove from the pan.

Yield:12 muffins

TIP: Fill empty muffin cups halfway with water to prevent the pan from warping.

DAIRY-FREE MUFFINS

These muffins are moist without the use of eggs or cow's milk. You can substitute soy milk, coconut milk, or rice milk for the almond milk, if you prefer.

1-1/2 cups whole wheat pastry flour
1/4 cup flaxseed meal
1 cup rolled oats
1-1/2 teaspoons baking powder
1/2 teaspoon baking soda
1/2 teaspoon salt
1 cup dried fruit or chocolate chips
2 tablespoons coconut oil, softened
1/3 cup brown sugar
1/4 cup agave nectar or honey
1/2 teaspoon stevia glycerite or 1/2 cup evaporated cane sugar
3/4 cup unsweetened applesauce
3/4 cup almond milk

Preheat oven to 350 degrees. Coat a 12-cup muffin pan with cooking spray.
In a large bowl, mix the flour, flaxseed meal, oats, baking powder, baking soda, and salt. Add dried fruit and stir.

In a separate bowl, stir the coconut oil until creamy. Whisk in the brown sugar and agave then add stevia, applesauce, and milk. Stir well to mix. Add wet ingredients to dry and stir just until moistened. Spoon batter into the prepared muffin pan and bake for 18-20 minutes or until tops begin to brown and a toothpick comes out clean.

Yield: 12 muffins

TIP: Coconut oil will form small, hard lumps if mixed directly with cold ingredients. When using coconut oil in baking, combine the coconut oil with the sugar, or room temperature agave nectar, whisk until creamy, then add the remaining wet ingredients and whisk vigorously.

FRUIT 'N' BRAN MUFFINS

These muffins are low in sugar and high in fiber. If using coconut oil, make sure that the agave and egg are at room temperature or warm, to avoid hard oil lumps.

2 cups whole wheat pastry flour
1/2 cup quick oats
2 tablespoons flaxseed meal
1/4 cup wheat germ
1 cup wheat bran
3/4 teaspoon salt
1 tablespoon baking powder
1 teaspoon baking soda
1 cup dried fruit (raisins, chopped dates, or cranberries)
2 tablespoons coconut oil or butter, softened
2 tablespoons brown sugar
1/2 cup agave nectar or honey, at room temperature
1 egg, room temperature
3 tablespoons apple juice
3/4 cup unsweetened applesauce
3/4 teaspoon stevia glycerite or 3/4 cup brown sugar
1–1/4 cups milk

Preheat oven to 350 degrees. Coat a 12-cup muffin pan with cooking spray.

In a large bowl, mix the flour, oats, flaxseed meal, wheat germ, wheat bran, salt, baking powder, baking soda, and raisins. In a separate bowl, whisk the coconut oil, brown sugar, and agave until creamy. Add the egg, apple juice, applesauce, stevia, and milk, and blend well. Add wet ingredients to dry and stir just until moistened.

Spoon the batter into the prepared muffin pan and bake for 18-20 minutes or until a toothpick comes out clean. Let cool for 5 minutes then remove from the pan.

Yield: 12 muffins

TIP: To avoid pointy, tough muffins, do not overmix the batter. Mix wet and dry ingredients just until moistened.

ZUCCHINI OATMEAL MUFFINS

This recipe makes a large batch of muffins. Use 2 muffin pans or make 12 muffins and a small loaf.

3/4 cup buttermilk (or 3/4 cup milk plus 2 teaspoons lemon juice)
1 tablespoon softened coconut oil, butter or unrefined canola oil
1/2 cup evaporated cane sugar
1/4 teaspoon stevia glycerite or increase sugar to 3/4 cup
1 egg, at room temperature
3/4 cup unsweetened applesauce
1/3 cup agave nectar or honey
1/4 teaspoon freshly grated lemon peel
1 cup grated zucchini
2 cups whole wheat pastry flour
3/4 teaspoon salt
3/4 teaspoon baking soda
3/4 teaspoon baking powder
1 cup rolled oats
1 teaspoon cinnamon
1/2 teaspoon nutmeg
3/4 cup chocolate chips or raisins(optional)

Preheat oven to 350 degrees. Grease 18 muffin cups or 12 muffin cups and 1 small loaf pan. Mix milk and lemon juice in a small bowl and set aside for 10 minutes (if not using buttermilk).

In a large bowl, whisk the coconut oil, sugar and stevia until well mixed. Add the egg, applesauce, agave, and lemon peel, and whisk vigorously. Gently stir in the zucchini. In a separate bowl, mix the flour, salt, baking soda, baking powder, oats, cinnamon, nutmeg, and chocolate chips. Add wet ingredients to dry and stir just until moistened.

Spoon batter into the prepared muffin pan and bake for 20 minutes or until a toothpick comes out clean. Remove from the oven, let cool for 5 minutes, then remove from the pan.

Yield: 18 muffins

TIP: If using honey and oil in a recipe, measure the oil first so that when you measure the honey, it won't stick to the measuring cup.

OATMEAL CHOCOLATE CHIP MUFFINS

This is a delicious, moist muffin that is simple to make. I like to use a combination of chocolate chips, peanut butter chips and raisins instead of just chocolate chips.

1-1/4 cups quick oats
1-1/2 cups boiling water
1-1/2 cups whole wheat pastry flour
1/2 cup brown sugar
1-1/2 teaspoons baking powder
3/4 teaspoon baking soda
1 teaspoon salt
1/2 teaspoon cinnamon
3/4 cup chocolate chips
1 egg
1/2 cup unsweetened applesauce
1/4 cup agave nectar or honey
1/4 teaspoon stevia glycerite or increase brown sugar to 3/4 cup
1 teaspoon pure vanilla extract
1/4 cup milk

Preheat oven to 350 degrees. Spray a 12-cup muffin pan with cooking spray.

Combine oats and boiling water in a bowl and set aside. In a large bowl, mix the flour, sugar, baking powder, baking soda, salt, cinnamon, and chocolate chips. In a separate bowl mix the egg, applesauce, agave, stevia, vanilla, and milk then stir in the oats. Add dry ingredients to wet and stir just until moistened.

Bake for 20 minutes or until a toothpick comes out clean. Let cool for 5 minutes, then remove from the pan.

For <u>Oatmeal Blueberry Muffins:</u> Replace chocolate chips with frozen blueberries.

Yield: 12 muffins

TIP: Toss dried fruit and chocolate chips with a small amount of flour before adding to a muffin or cake batter (or mix directly with the dry ingredients). This will help prevent the fruit or chocolate chips from sinking to the bottom while baking.

PUMPKIN CARROT JAM MUFFINS

Kids love to find the sweet jam surprise when they bite into this muffin.

2 cups whole wheat pastry flour
2 tablespoons flaxseed meal or wheat germ
2 teaspoons baking powder
1/2 teaspoon baking soda
2 teaspoons cinnamon
1 teaspoon ground ginger
1/4 teaspoon ground nutmeg
1 teaspoon salt
1 tablespoon butter or coconut oil, softened
2/3 cup brown sugar
1/4 teaspoon stevia glycerite or increase brown sugar by 1/4 cup
1/2 cup unsweetened applesauce
1/2 cup honey or agave nectar
2 eggs
1 teaspoon pure vanilla extract
1 cup shredded carrots
1 cup pureed pumpkin
1/2 cup chopped large dates, stems and pits removed (about 5 dates)
1/4 cup fruit juice-sweetened jam

Preheat oven to 350 degrees. Grease a 12-cup muffin pan.

In a large bowl mix flour, flaxseed meal, baking powder, baking soda, cinnamon, ginger, nutmeg, and salt. In a separate bowl whisk butter and sugar together. Add stevia, applesauce, honey, eggs, and vanilla; stir well. Mix in carrot, pumpkin, and dates, add the wet ingredients to the dry and stir just until mixed. Fill muffin tins half full of batter. Add a teaspoon of jam and then scoop more batter on top.

Bake for 20 minutes or until a toothpick comes out clean. Remove from the oven and let cool for 5 minutes before removing from the pan.

Yield: 12 muffins

TIP: If you can't find flaxseed meal, grind whole flaxseeds in a dry coffee grinder until powdered.

STRAWBERRY BANANA MUFFINS

1-3/4 cups whole wheat pastry flour
1-1/2 teaspoons baking powder
3/4 teaspoon baking soda
1/2 teaspoon salt
1/2 teaspoon cinnamon
1 cup rolled oats
1 tablespoon toasted wheat germ
1/4 cup plus 1 tablespoon evaporated cane sugar
1/4 cup plain low-fat yogurt
1/2 teaspoon stevia glycerite or increase sugar to 3/4 cup
2 eggs or 1 egg and 2 egg whites, lightly beaten
3/4 cup milk
1 teaspoon pure vanilla extract
1 banana, mashed
1-1/4 cups fresh or frozen and thawed strawberries, sliced (or blueberries)

Preheat oven to 350 degrees. Spray a 12-cup muffin pan with cooking spray.

In a large bowl combine the flour, baking powder, baking soda, salt, cinnamon, oats, wheat germ, and sugar; stir to mix. In a separate bowl, mix the yogurt, stevia, eggs, milk, and vanilla. Stir in the banana then add the wet ingredients to the dry. Stir just until moistened then gently stir in the berries.

Spoon batter into muffin cups and bake for 20-25 minutes or until a toothpick comes out clean. Let cool for 5 minutes before removing.

Yield: 12 muffins

TIP: Freeze cooled baked goods in an airtight container for up to 3 months. Thaw cookies or muffins as needed.

BRAN MUFFINS

These muffins are a great on-the-go snack. They are high in fiber which helps to keep your blood sugar stable. They will keep you full and satisfied.

1–1/2 cups bran cereal
1 cup wheat bran
3/4 cup apple juice
2 cups whole wheat pastry flour
1 tablespoon flaxseed meal
3/4 cup brown sugar
1 tablespoon baking powder
1/2 teaspoon baking soda
1/2 teaspoon salt
1 egg
1 teaspoon pure vanilla extract
1/4 teaspoon stevia glycerite (or increase brown sugar to 1 cup)
1/2 cup agave nectar or honey
1/4 cup molasses or increase agave to 3/4 cup
1 cup raisins
1 cup buttermilk (or 1 cup milk and 1 tablespoon lemon juice)

Preheat oven to 350 degrees. Grease a 12-cup muffin pan. Mix the milk and lemon juice and set aside for 10 minutes, if not using buttermilk.

In a large bowl combine the bran cereal, wheat bran, and apple juice and let sit for at least 5 minutes. In a separate large bowl, mix the flour, flaxseed meal, brown sugar, baking powder, baking soda, and salt. Add egg, vanilla, stevia, agave, molasses, and raisins to the bran mixture then stir in the buttermilk. Add the wet mixture to the dry and stir just until moistened.

Scoop batter evenly into the prepared muffin pan. Bake for 20-25 minutes or until a toothpick comes out clean. Let cool for 5 minutes before removing from the pan.

Yield: 12 muffins

TIP: If you don't have buttermilk, make a substitute by mixing 1 cup milk with 1 tablespoon lemon juice. Let sit for 5-10 minutes before using.

PUMPKIN CREAM CHEESE LOAF

This is a not-too-sweet pumpkin bread with a sweet cheese surprise in the middle.

Pumpkin Batter:
1 cup canned pumpkin
1/2 cup evaporated cane sugar
1/2 cup brown sugar
1/2 cup agave nectar or honey
1 egg
1 egg white
1 cup milk
1/4 cup unsweetened applesauce
1 cup whole wheat flour or whole wheat pastry flour
1 cup unbleached all purpose flour
2-1/2 teaspoons baking powder
2 teaspoons pumpkin pie spice
1/2 teaspoon cinnamon
1/4 teaspoon salt

Cream Cheese Filling:
1 (8-ounce) package reduced-fat cream cheese, softened
2 tablespoons evaporated cane sugar
1 egg white

Preheat oven to 350 degrees. Grease an 8 by 4 by 2 inch loaf pan or 2 smaller loaf pans.

In a large bowl, mix the pumpkin, sugars, agave, egg, 1 egg white, milk, and applesauce. Add the flour, baking powder, pumpkin pie spice, cinnamon, and salt. Stir just until moistened and set aside. In a medium bowl, beat the cream cheese, 2 tablespoons sugar and the second egg white until well blended. Spoon half of the pumpkin batter into the prepared pan, spread the cream cheese mixture evenly over the batter, then cover with the remaining pumpkin batter.

Bake for about 1 hour for a large loaf or 35 minutes for small loaves or until a toothpick comes out clean. Cool in the pan for 15 minutes then run a spatula or knife around the edges of the pan to loosen the loaf. Remove loaf from pan, transfer to a wire rack, and let cool completely.

Yield: 12 servings

TIP: Keep a mixture of flaxseed meal and wheat germ in a sealed container in the fridge or freezer. For a simple way to increase the nutrition of foods, add a few tablespoons to muffins, pancakes, breads, and breading.

ZUCCHINI PINEAPPLE LOAF

This loaf is light in texture and sweetness.

2 eggs
1/2 cup agave nectar or honey
1/2 cup evaporated cane sugar
1/4 teaspoon stevia glycerite or increase sugar to 3/4 cup
1 cup grated zucchini
1 cup crushed pineapple, drained
2 cups whole wheat pastry flour
1 teaspoon baking soda
1/2 teaspoon baking powder
1/2 teaspoon salt
3/4 teaspoon cinnamon
1/2 teaspoon ground nutmeg
1/2 cup raisins or chopped nuts(optional)

Preheat oven to 350 degrees. Grease an 8 by 4 by 2 inch loaf pan and set aside.

In a large bowl, mix the eggs, agave, sugar, and stevia then stir in the zucchini and pineapple. In a separate bowl combine the flour, baking soda, baking powder, salt, cinnamon, nutmeg, and raisins and stir to mix. Add the wet ingredients to the dry and stir just until combined. Pour batter into the loaf pan and bake for 45 minutes or until a toothpick comes out clean. Let cool for 15 minutes then run a knife along the edge of the loaf to loosen. Remove from the pan and set on a wire rack to cool completely.

Yield: 12 servings

For Zucchini Chocolate Chip Loaf: Omit the pineapple and nutmeg. Add 3/4 cup unsweetened applesauce and 1/2 cup chocolate chips.

TIP: If the top of a quickbread loaf is browning too quickly, cover it with nonstick aluminum foil then remove for the last 15 minutes of baking.

CINNAMON SUGAR BANANA BREAD

This bread tastes sinfully delicious but is lower in fat and sugar than traditional banana bread.

1/4 cup softened butter or coconut oil (or 2 tablespoons of each)
1/4 cup unsweetened applesauce
2 eggs or 1 egg and 2 egg whites
1/4 cup agave nectar or honey
1/2 cup brown sugar
1/4 teaspoon stevia glycerite or increase sugar to 3/4 cup
1 cup mashed banana (2 large bananas)
1-3/4 cups whole wheat pastry flour
2 tablespoons wheat germ or flaxseed meal
2 teaspoons baking powder
1/2 teaspoon baking soda
1/4 teaspoon salt
1/4 cup chopped walnuts (optional)
1/4 cup chocolate chips (optional)
1/2 teaspoon cinnamon
2 tablespoons brown sugar

Preheat oven to 350 degrees. Grease an 8 by 4 by 2 inch loaf pan.

In a large bowl, mix the butter, applesauce, eggs, agave, 1/2 cup brown sugar, and stevia until smooth then stir in the banana. Combine the flour, wheat germ, baking powder, baking soda, salt, walnuts, and chocolate chips in a separate large bowl. Measure the remaining 2 tablespoons brown sugar and the cinnamon into a small bowl and set aside. Add wet ingredients to dry and stir just until combined. Pour half of batter into the prepared pan, sprinkle cinnamon sugar onto batter then top with the rest of the batter.

Bake for 40-50 minutes or until a toothpick comes out clean. Set the pan on a wire rack to cool for 15 minutes, run a knife along the outside edge to loosen, then remove from pan and let cool completely.

Yield: 12 servings

TIP: *Baked goods using coconut oil tend to be slightly more crumbly than using just butter. Use half organic butter and half coconut oil in baked goods to retain the benefits of the coconut oil, and the taste and texture of butter.*

PUMPKIN BREAD

1-1/4 cups whole wheat pastry flour
1/4 cup wheat germ or flaxseed meal
1 teaspoon baking powder
1/4 teaspoon baking soda
1/4 teaspoon salt
1/2 cup brown sugar
1/4 teaspoon stevia glycerite or increase brown sugar to 3/4 cup
1/3 cup agave nectar or honey
1/3 cup unsweetened applesauce
1/4 cup milk
1-1/4 cups canned pumpkin (or fresh, cooked and pureed)
1 egg
1 teaspoon pure vanilla extract
1/4 cup chopped fruit (apples or dates), chocolate chips, or raisins

Preheat oven to 350 degrees. Spray an 8 by 4 by 2 inch loaf pan with cooking spray.

In a large mixing bowl, mix the flour, wheat germ, baking powder, baking soda, and salt. In a separate bowl, mix the brown sugar, stevia, and agave together then add the applesauce, milk, pumpkin, egg, and vanilla. Mix well then add the wet ingredients to the dry. Stir to combine, then stir in the fruit or chocolate chips.

Bake for 45 -55 minutes or until a toothpick comes out clean. Let cool for 10 minutes, run a knife around the loaf, then remove from the pan. Let cool completely on a wire rack.

Yield:12 servings

TIP: *If your loaves have an indentation in the middle after baking, they are rising too quickly and then falling. Decrease the amount of baking soda or baking powder, or increase the amount of flour used, to have nicely rounded loaves.*

CHICKEN DISHES

Chicken Parmesan

Sesame Sweet Chicken

Spinach and Cheese Stuffed Chicken Breasts with White Wine Reduction

Chicken Marsala

Apricot Chicken

Cinnamon Glazed Chicken

Tequila Lime Chicken Fajitas with Lime Dressing

Chicken Lettuce Wraps

Chicken Quesadillas

Crispy Baked Chicken

CHAPTER FIVE

CHICKEN PARMESAN

This delicious, hearty chicken dish is lower in fat than the typical version. It is lightened up by cooking the chicken in a small amount of oil then finishes cooking in the oven. The whole wheat bread crumbs and wheat germ give the dish a nutrition boost.

4 boneless skinless chicken breasts (about 2 pounds)
1/4 cup unbleached all purpose flour
1/4 teaspoon salt
1/8 teaspoon black pepper
2 eggs, lightly beaten
1/4 cup water or milk
1 cup dry whole wheat bread crumbs
1 tablespoon wheat germ or flaxseed meal
1/4 cup grated Parmesan cheese
1/2 teaspoon garlic salt
1/2 teaspoon salt
1 teaspoon dried basil
1 teaspoon dried oregano
1 teaspoon dried parsley
1 (32-ounce) jar organic pasta sauce or 4 cups homemade Pasta Sauce (see index)
1–2 cups shredded mozzarella cheese
Extra virgin olive oil or grapeseed oil for frying

Preheat oven to 350 degrees.

Place one chicken breast between 2 pieces of folded plastic wrap, or in a plastic bag. Flatten the chicken to 1/2-inch thickness with the flat side of a meat mallet. Repeat with the remaining pieces of chicken. Measure the flour into a flat dish and season the flour with salt and pepper. Mix the eggs and water in a separate dish. Combine the bread crumbs, wheat germ, Parmesan, garlic salt, salt, basil, oregano and parsley in a third dish.

Heat 1 tablespoon olive oil in a large skillet on medium heat. One at a time, dip the chicken in the flour, then the egg, then coat in the bread crumbs. Place 1-2 pieces of chicken in the hot frying pan. Cook chicken 1-2 pieces at a time, adding more oil if the chicken begins to stick. Cook for 3-4 minutes per side or until golden brown. Repeat the process with remaining pieces of chicken. In a 9 by 13 glass dish, spread 1/2 cup pasta sauce to lightly coat the bottom. Place browned chicken breasts on top of sauce. Top each piece of chicken with a few tablespoons of pasta sauce and 1/4 cup –1/2 cup mozzarella.

Bake chicken for 30 minutes or until the chicken is cooked through and the cheese is lightly browned. Serve over whole wheat noodles and warm pasta sauce.

Yield: 4-6 servings

SWEET SESAME CHICKEN

1 pound mixed chicken pieces (4–6 pieces)
3 tablespoons brown sugar
1/4 cup honey
2 tablespoons soy sauce or tamari
1 tablespoon lime juice
1 teaspoon freshly grated ginger
1 tablespoon sesame seeds

Preheat oven to 350 degrees.

In a small bowl, combine the sugar, honey, soy sauce, lime juice, grated ginger, and sesame seeds. Stir to mix. Pour the marinade into a large resealable plastic bag and add the chicken. Seal bag and shake to coat, then refrigerate for least an hour, turning the bag 2-3 times. Remove the chicken from the bag and discard the marinade. Bake the chicken in the oven or cook on a preheated grill until cooked through (approximately 20 minutes).

Yield. 4 servings

TIP: Buy firm ginger root with the least amount of knobs and/or branching. Ginger root will keep for up to 3 months in the freezer. Two options to freeze are the following: peel the whole root and store in a resealable plastic freezer bag, remove from the freezer, grate as needed and refreeze the root OR the entire root can be peeled and minced, then frozen in small portions using an ice cube tray; remove and thaw portions as needed.

SPINACH AND CHEESE STUFFED CHICKEN BREASTS WITH WHITE WINE REDUCTION

The tangy cheese and the sweet wine glaze are delicious together in this tender chicken dish. This meal will impress your guests. It seems gourmet but is simple to prepare. For variety, soak sun-dried tomatoes in hot water for 10 minutes, drain and dice, then use in place of the dried cranberries.

White Wine Reduction:
1/2 cup white wine (dry or sweet)
1/2 cup red wine vinegar or white wine vinegar
3 tablespoons agave nectar or honey

Stuffed Chicken:
1–2 tablespoons coconut oil or extra virgin olive oil
4 boneless skinless chicken breasts (about 2 pounds)
Salt and pepper
6 tablespoons goat cheese or Boursin cheese
2 tablespoons dried cranberries, chopped
2 cups packed fresh baby spinach
1/4 cup white wine
1 tablespoon agave nectar or honey

Preheat oven to 350 degrees.

Prepare the white wine reduction: Pour 1/2 cup white wine, vinegar, and agave into a small saucepan, stir thoroughly, and set on medium-high heat. When the mixture begins to bubble, reduce heat to medium-low and simmer for about 30-45 minutes or until reduced to about 1/4 cup. While the sauce is reducing, prepare the chicken.

Place a chicken breast between two sheets of folded plastic wrap, or in a plastic bag. Flatten to 1/4-inch thickness using the flat side of a meat mallet. Transfer chicken to a flat dish and set aside. Repeat with remaining 3 chicken breasts.

In a bowl, mash the cheese with a fork; add the cranberries and stir well. Salt and pepper both sides of each piece of chicken. Place 1-1/2 tablespoons of the cheese mixture in the center of each piece of chicken. Place 1/4 cup of fresh spinach leaves on top of the cheese, fold each piece of chicken over and secure with a toothpick.

Heat 1/2 tablespoon of coconut oil in a large skillet over medium-high heat. Cook 2 chicken breasts for 3-4 minutes per side or until golden brown then transfer to an oven-safe baking dish. Repeat with remaining chicken, adding more oil if needed. Mix 1/4 cup white wine with one tablespoon of agave; stir to combine, and pour into the bottom of the chicken dish. Cover the dish with aluminum foil, bake for 15 minutes, remove foil and cook for 5-10 more minutes or until the chicken is cooked through. Remove from the oven and take out the toothpicks.

Once the pan sauce has reduced, remove from the heat to let cool slightly. To serve, transfer the chicken to a serving platter and drizzle sauce on top. Serve with cooked brown rice or polenta.

Yield: 4 servings

CHICKEN MARSALA

4 boneless skinless chicken breasts
1/4 cup unbleached all purpose flour
1/2 teaspoon salt
1/8 teaspoon freshly ground black pepper
1/2 teaspoon dried oregano
1-2 tablespoons coconut oil
1-2 tablespoons butter
1-1/2 cups fresh button mushrooms, quartered
1/2 cup yellow onion, cut into 1/2-inch thick slices
1 cup Marsala wine
1 cup chicken broth
2 teaspoons cornstarch or arrowroot

Place one chicken breast between two pieces of wax paper, or plastic wrap. Pound with a meat mallet until chicken is 1/4 -1/2 inch thick. Repeat with remaining chicken breasts and set aside.

In a shallow dish, mix the flour, salt, pepper, and oregano. In a large frying pan, heat 1/2 tablespoon oil and 1/2 tablespoon butter on medium heat-high. Coat chicken in the flour mixture and shake off excess. Place 2 chicken breasts in the hot skillet and cook for 3-4 minutes per side or until browned. Transfer to a plate then repeat with the other chicken breasts, adding oil and butter as needed. In a small bowl, mix 1/2 cup chicken broth with cornstarch and set aside.

In the same frying pan, cook the mushrooms and onion on medium heat for 2 minutes. Add Marsala wine and the remaining 1/2 cup of chicken broth and simmer for 5 minutes. Return chicken to the pan and add broth/cornstarch mixture. Bring to a boil, reduce heat to medium-low, and simmer until the chicken is cooked through and the sauce has thickened. Transfer chicken to a serving plate and pour sauce on top.

Serve with whole wheat pasta and Garlic Broccoli (see index).

Yield: 4 servings

TIP: To brown mushrooms, heat a skillet with a small amount of oil, add mushrooms and let them cook for a few minutes before stirring or seasoning with salt. Adding salt too soon will draw out the water and result in too much liquid in the pan to allow the mushrooms to brown.

APRICOT CHICKEN

For Peach Chicken, substitute 1/4 cup sliced canned peaches for the apricots. If you don't have fennel, use sliced yellow onion instead.

Coconut oil or extra virgin olive oil for sautéing
4 boneless skinless chicken breasts
Salt and black pepper
2 tablespoons Anaheim or Poblano pepper, finely chopped or 1/4 teaspoon hot sauce
2 green onions, sliced into 1/2-inch pieces
1 fennel bulb
1 cup orange juice
3 tablespoons apricot jam (fruit juice sweetened)
1/4 cup chopped dried apricots (about 5)
1 teaspoon lemon juice
1 tablespoon arrowroot or non-GMO cornstarch
2 tablespoons fresh parsley, chopped

In a large frying pan, heat 1 teaspoon of oil on medium-high heat. Season both sides of each piece of chicken with salt and pepper. Cook the chicken for 4-5 minutes per side or until golden brown, then transfer to a plate. This may need to be done in batches, adding more oil as needed.

Cut fennel bulb in half lengthwise, remove and discard the core, then slice the remaining fennel and set aside. In the same frying pan as the chicken was cooked in, add 1 teaspoon oil and set on medium heat. Cook the Anaheim pepper, onions, and fennel for 2 minutes until they start to brown. Add 3/4 cup orange juice, apricot jam, apricots, and lemon juice and let simmer for a few minutes. In a small bowl, mix cornstarch with remaining 1/4 cup orange juice then pour into pan. Stir thoroughly. Add the chicken, reduce the heat to medium-low and cover the pan with a lid. Let simmer for 10 minutes, flip chicken over and cook for another 5-10 minutes until chicken is completely cooked. Season with salt and pepper to taste. Remove chicken from the pan and transfer to a serving dish.

To serve, place chicken on top of cooked brown rice, pour apricot sauce on top, and garnish with parsley.

Yield: 4 servings

TIP: To prevent chicken from sticking to the pan, add oil to a skillet and set heat to medium-high. Make sure that the pan is hot before adding the chicken. Let the chicken cook for a few minutes before moving it around. If you attempt to move it too soon it will stick to the pan.

CINNAMON GLAZED CHICKEN

This simple glaze tastes great on grilled or baked chicken. As a kid, it was my job to prepare the cinnamon-honey glaze for my dad while he was grilling.

1 pound chicken pieces (4–6 pieces)
Salt and pepper
1 cup agave nectar or honey
3 teaspoons ground cinnamon

Preheat oven to 375 degrees or heat a grill to medium-high heat.

Sprinkle all sides of chicken with salt and pepper. Mix agave and cinnamon in a small bowl and set aside. Bake or grill chicken for 10 minutes. Baste chicken with cinnamon-agave mixture, cook for 5 minutes, turn pieces over then baste other side. Continue to cook until chicken is no longer pink, basting frequently. Discard remaining glaze. Transfer chicken to a plate and serve with cooked quinoa or brown rice, and a big green salad.

Yield: 4 servings

TEQUILA LIME CHICKEN FAJITAS
WITH LIME DRESSING

Chicken:
4 boneless skinless chicken breasts
2 tablespoons tequila
1/4 cup fresh lime juice
2 tablespoons extra virgin olive oil
1/3 cup agave nectar or honey
1/8 teaspoon black pepper
3 cloves garlic, minced (or 1 tablespoon)
2 teaspoons dried oregano
1/2 red bell pepper
1/2 green bell pepper
1/2 yellow bell pepper
1 red onion, cut into 1/4-inch slices
8 (8-inch) whole wheat flour or sprouted grain tortillas
Sour cream/shredded cheddar cheese/salsa/guacamole/refried beans for topping

Veggie Dressing:
1/4 cup agave nectar, honey, or maple syrup
2 tablespoons lime juice
1 teaspoon garlic salt
1/. teaspoon salt
1/8 teaspoon black pepper
1 teaspoon dried oregano
1 tablespoon extra virgin olive oil

Place a chicken breast between 2 pieces of folded plastic wrap, or in a plastic bag. Flatten chicken to 1/2-inch thickness using the flat side of a meat mallet. Repeat with remaining chicken breasts and transfer to a large resealable plastic bag.

In a small bowl, mix tequila, lime juice, olive oil, agave, pepper, garlic, and oregano. Stir to combine then pour over the chicken. Seal the bag and turn it over several times to coat the chicken. Refrigerate for at least 1 hour.

Prepare and cook the vegetables. Cut the bell peppers into 1/2-inch strips, transfer to a greased cookie sheet then add the sliced onions. Spray the vegetables with cooking spray, sprinkle lightly with salt, then bake for 15 minutes. Broil for the last 3 minutes to char slightly. Cook the chicken while the vegetables are roasting.

Preheat a grill to medium-high heat. Remove chicken from bag and discard marinade. Grill chicken for 5 minutes, turn over, then cook until the chicken is no longer pink. Transfer to a plate and cut into 1/2-inch strips. Prepare the veggie dressing while the chicken is cooking.

In a small bowl stir together the agave, lime juice, garlic salt, salt, pepper and oregano. Add the oil, stir, and set aside. Remove the cooked veggies from the oven, transfer to a bowl, pour veggie dressing on top and stir to coat. Set a tortilla on a flat surface, add chicken and veggies and your favorite toppings. Tuck in sides and roll up.

Yield: 8 servings

TIP: Before cooking meat on the grill or stovetop or oven, remove it from the fridge and allow it to rest for 10-15 minutes. Meat will seize up and be tough if cooked directly from the fridge.

CHICKEN LETTUCE WRAPS

This is one of my favorite restaurant appetizers so I created my own homemade version. There are several ingredients but these wraps are really simple and quick to prepare.

Stir-fry Sauce:
4 tablespoons brown sugar
4 tablespoons soy sauce
1 teaspoon brown rice vinegar
2 teaspoons arrowroot or non-GMO cornstarch

Chicken Mixture:
Cooking spray or 2 teaspoons coconut oil or extra virgin olive oil
1 pound ground chicken breast or 2-3 diced boneless skinless chicken breasts
1 tablespoon minced garlic
1/2 teaspoon minced or finely diced ginger
1/2 cup diced carrots
1/4 cup chopped red bell pepper
2 green onions, sliced into 1/2-inch pieces
1/2 cup mushrooms, chopped
3/4 cup water chestnuts, drained and chopped
1 head iceberg, green leaf, or Bibb lettuce, washed and separated into whole leaves

Sauce:
1/2 cup agave nectar or honey or 1/4 cup brown sugar
2 tablespoons soy sauce or tamari
2 tablespoons brown rice vinegar
2 tablespoons ketchup
1 tablespoon lemon juice
2 teaspoons prepared Dijon mustard or hot mustard
2 teaspoons minced garlic
1/4 teaspoon sesame oil
1-2 teaspoons chili garlic sauce or crushed red pepper flakes

In a small bowl, mix the brown sugar, soy sauce, rice vinegar, and arrowroot. Stir until the sugar dissolves then set aside.

In a large frying pan, heat the oil on medium-low heat. Add the chicken and stir-fry sauce and stir to break the chicken into pieces. Cook the meat for 2-3 minutes, stirring often, then add the garlic, ginger, carrots, red bell pepper, green onions, mushrooms, and water chestnuts. Continue to cook for about 5 more minutes or until the meat is cooked and vegetables are tender.

While the chicken is cooking, prepare the sauce. Mix the agave, soy sauce, brown rice vinegar, ketchup, lemon juice, mustard, garlic, sesame oil and chili garlic sauce in a small bowl. Stir and set aside.

To assemble, place a lettuce leaf on a plate, spoon 1/2 cup chicken mixture on top, then add sauce, or pour sauce in a bowl for dipping.

Yield: 6 servings

CHICKEN QUESADILLAS

One of my friends favorite dishes to make is chicken quesadillas. I borrowed the idea to put the salsa inside the quesadilla from her.

8 (10-inch) whole wheat flour or sprouted grain tortillas
2 boneless skinless chicken breasts, diced
2 teaspoons extra virgin olive oil
1 teaspoon ground cumin
1 teaspoon dried oregano
1 teaspoon garlic salt
1 cup salsa
1-2 cups shredded mozzarella cheese
2 cups Monterey Jack or cheddar cheese
Sour cream and avocado for garnish

In a medium frying pan, heat the olive oil on medium heat. Add the chicken to the pan and sprinkle with cumin, oregano and garlic salt. Cook chicken for 5 minutes or until cooked through; stir often. Add more oil if needed. Add the salsa, 1/2 cup mozzarella and 1/2 cup Monterey Jack to the pan and stir until the cheese melts.

Heat a separate large frying pan on medium heat and place a flour tortilla in the pan. Place 1/2 cup chicken mixture on top. Top with 1/2-1 cup mixed cheeses then top with remaining tortilla. Cook for 5 minutes or until the cheese begins to melt and the bottom tortilla is lightly browned. Gently flip to cook the other side until lightly browned. Repeat with remaining tortillas.

The quesadillas can be baked instead of heating in a frying pan. To bake, assemble the four quesadillas on a lightly greased baking sheet. Bake at 350 degrees for 10 minutes or until the cheese is melted.

Transfer to a plate and cut each quesadilla into 4 pieces. Top with a dollop of sour cream and sliced avocado.

Yield: 8 servings, 1/2 quesadilla each

CRISPY BAKED CHICKEN

This recipe proves that it is easy to make delicious, crispy chicken without deep frying. Soaking the chicken in buttermilk helps it to tenderize. You can skip this step and simply dip the chicken in the egg mixture and bread crumbs if you don't have buttermilk. Feel free to use 1 pound of drumsticks or thighs instead of breasts, just add a few minutes cooking time.

1 pound boneless skinless chicken breasts (2 large or 3 medium breasts)
1-1/2 cups buttermilk
1/4 cup unbleached all purpose flour
1 large egg and 1 egg white or 3 egg whites, lightly beaten
1 cup whole wheat or Panko (Japanese) bread crumbs or 1/2 cup bread crumbs and 1/2 cup crushed cornflake cereal
1/4 cup toasted wheat germ or flaxseed meal
1 teaspoon garlic powder
1/2 teaspoon paprika
3/4 teaspoon salt
1/2 teaspoon onion powder
2 tablespoons grated Parmesan cheese
1-2 tablespoons coconut oil or grapeseed oil
Cooking spray

Cut chicken breasts into 1/4-inch thick strips (4-5 strips per breast). Combine the chicken and buttermilk in a shallow dish or resealable plastic bag. Seal tightly, shake to coat, and chill for 1 hour.

Combine the egg and egg white in a flat-bottomed dish. In a separate dish combine the bread crumbs, wheat germ, garlic powder, paprika, salt, onion powder, and Parmesan cheese.

Preheat oven to 425 degrees. Remove chicken from the marinade, transfer to a bowl and discard the liquid. Combine the flour and chicken in the bowl and toss to coat evenly. One strip or piece at a time, dip chicken in the egg mixture then toss gently in the bread crumbs to coat.

While breading the chicken, brush 1-2 tablespoons of coconut oil or grapeseed oil onto a baking sheet and place in the oven. Let the pan heat for 3-5 minutes before removing. Arrange chicken in a single layer on the preheated baking sheet. Generously coat chicken with cooking spray and bake for 6 minutes, turn pieces over and cook for 4-6 minutes or until cooked through. Serve with Honey Mustard Sauce(see index), Honey Barbeque Sauce (see index) or store-bought barbeque sauce.

Yield: 12-15 chicken strips. Serves: 4

Options: This dish can be made easily if you use pre-made Crispy Coating (see index). Use 1-1/2 cups of the Crispy Coating to replace the bread crumbs, wheat germ, seasonings, and Parmesan cheese in this recipe.

For <u>Coconut Chicken Fingers:</u> Decrease bread crumbs to 3/4 cup. Add 3/4 cup flaked coconut, 1/2 teaspoon curry powder, and a dash of cayenne pepper. Serve with Apricot-Dijon Dipping Sauce (see index).

For <u>Crispy Shrimp:</u> Replace the chicken with 1 pound small shrimp, omit soaking in the buttermilk and reduce baking time to 5 minutes.

TIP: Japanese style coarse-ground Panko bread crumbs are great for fillers and breading because they tend to stay crispy longer and absorb less grease than regular bread crumbs. Substitute with regular bread crumbs if you don't have Panko bread crumbs.

MAIN DISHES

SWEET CHILE GLAZED MAHIMAHI

This is a mildly spicy and sweet glaze that tastes delicious on mahimahi, tilapia, or salmon.

4 fish fillets (16–20 ounces)

Glaze:
1 tablespoon minced garlic (about 3 cloves)
1 tablespoon chili powder
3/4 teaspoon salt
1–1/2 teaspoons onion powder
3 tablespoons brown sugar
1–1/2 teaspoons extra virgin olive oil
1 tablespoon Worcestershire sauce
6 tablespoons agave nectar or honey
Dash hot sauce or cayenne pepper

Preheat a grill to medium-high heat.

Mix the minced garlic, chili powder, salt, onion powder, brown sugar, olive oil, Worcestershire sauce, agave, and hot sauce in a small bowl. Brush the glaze on one side of the fillet and place glaze side down on a preheated, greased grill. Brush glaze on top of the fish and cook on direct heat for 4 minutes. Flip fish and grill 4 more minutes until fish flakes easily.

To Broil Fish: Glaze one side of fish and broil in the oven for 4 minutes, turn fish over, glaze the other side then broil another 4 minutes or until the fish is cooked and flakes easily.

Yield: 4 servings

SEARED SALMON WITH GARLIC SPINACH AND WHITE BEANS

White Beans:
2 teaspoons extra virgin olive oil
1 medium yellow onion, diced
1 (15-ounce) can cannellini beans
1/4 cup white wine
1 teaspoon dried parsley
Dash hot sauce
1/4 teaspoon salt
1/8 teaspoon freshly ground black pepper

Fish:
1 teaspoon extra virgin olive oil
4 (6-ounce) salmon fillets
Salt and pepper
Garlic powder

Garlic Spinach:
1 teaspoon extra virgin olive oil
1 tablespoon minced garlic (3 cloves)
8 cups packed baby spinach leaves
Salt and pepper
1 teaspoon lemon juice

In a large skillet or saucepan, heat the oil on medium heat. Cook and stir the onion for 10 minutes or until it begins to brown. Reduce heat to medium-low, add the beans, wine, parsley, hot sauce, salt, and pepper; stir and cook for a few more minutes then remove from the heat. Taste and adjust the salt and hot sauce to your liking.

To cook the salmon, season fillets with salt, pepper, and garlic powder. Heat 1 teaspoon olive oil on medium-high heat in a large skillet. When the oil is hot, add the salmon skin side down. Sear for 6 minutes, turn fish over, and cook for about another 5 minutes. While the salmon is cooking, prepare the spinach. Heat 1 teaspoon olive oil in a large saucepan. Add the garlic and cook on medium-low heat for 60 seconds. Add the spinach and cook for 2 minutes or until wilted; stir often. Season with salt and pepper, remove from heat and stir in the lemon juice.

To serve, scoop beans onto 4 plates, top with 1/2 cup cooked spinach and place a salmon fillet on top.

Yield: 4 servings

SHRIMP WITH TOMATOES AND FETA

4 teaspoons coconut oil
4 cloves garlic, minced
1/2 medium onion, diced (about 1/2 cup)
5 medium tomatoes, diced
2 dried ancho chilies (diced, seeds removed)
1 tablespoon dried thyme
1 tablespoon dried parsley
2 bay leaves
1 teaspoon salt
1/2 teaspoon black pepper
Dash hot sauce
2 teaspoons evaporated cane sugar
1 pound raw shrimp (peeled and deveined)
1 tablespoon fresh lime juic.
1/2 cup (2-ounces) feta cheese, crumbled
3 tablespoons chopped fresh cilantro

Melt 1-2 teaspoons of coconut oil in a large frying pan on medium heat. Cook and stir garlic and onion for 5 minutes or until the onion begins to soften. Add the tomatoes, chilies, thyme, parsley, bay leaves, salt, pepper, hot sauce, and sugar. Stir to combine, reduce heat to low, and let simmer for 10 minutes.

While the sauce is simmering, cook the shrimp. In a separate frying pan, melt 2 teaspoons of coconut oil on medium-high heat. Cook and stir the shrimp for a few minutes on each side to brown lightly. Add more oil if needed. Transfer shrimp to the tomato mixture, remove bay leaves, and cook for a few minutes more until they are cooked through. Remove from the heat; stir in 1/4 cup feta cheese and the lime juice. Pour the mixture into a serving bowl, sprinkle with the remaining feta and garnish with cilantro.

Serve with cooked brown rice or warm tortillas.

Yield: 4 servings

TIP: Cut fresh herbs easily using clean scissors. To freeze herbs, cut and place in a resealable plastic bag or plastic container with a lid. Remove as needed for recipes.

GLAZED PAN-FRIED TOFU

12 or 16 ounce block of extra firm tofu
2 tablespoons soy sauce or tamari
1/4 cup maple syrup
3 tablespoons mirin
1 teaspoon chili garlic sauce or 1/2 teaspoon crushed red pepper flakes
Coconut oil or peanut oil for frying

Set the block of tofu on a paper-towel-lined plate. Top with another piece of paper towel and then set a heavy dish or cast iron pan on top. Let sit for at least 30 minutes then discard the liquid from the bottom of the dish.

Mix the soy sauce, maple syrup, mirin, and chili garlic sauce in a bowl. Cut tofu into 1-inch cubes and place in a resealable plastic bag. Pour soy sauce marinade on top and seal the bag. Shake to coat tofu and refrigerate for 30 minutes to 1 hour, turning bag over occasionally. Remove the tofu from the fridge and set a colander on top of a large bowl. Dump tofu cubes into the colander to drain; reserve marinade for later.

Set a frying pan on medium-high heat and melt 1/2 tablespoon coconut oil. Place tofu in the skillet and cook for about 10 minutes, turning often to brown on all sides. Add 1/2 tablespoon more coconut oil at a time, if needed. Once all the tofu is browned on all sides, add the reserved marinade. Cook and stir for a few minutes until the tofu is coated and the sauce thickens a bit. Serve with brown rice and vegetables, or on top of the Asian Salad with Pan-Fried Glazed Tofu (see index).

Yield: 3-4 servings

TIP: Pressing the tofu reduces the liquid and provides for a firmer texture to the tofu when it is cooked.

BAKED FALAFEL

This is a delicious, meatless patty that is high in fiber and protein. It is a lighter version of the traditionally fried Middle Eastern dish with extra vegetables mixed in for added nutrition.

2 teaspoons extra virgin olive oil or coconut oil
1 large carrot, diced finely
1/2 medium yellow onion, finely diced (about 1/2 cup)
1 clove garlic, minced (about 1 teaspoon)
2 teaspoons ground cumin
1/2 teaspoon salt
1/8 teaspoon black pepper
1 (25-ounce) can garbanzo beans, lightly drained
2 tablespoons tahini (sesame seed paste)
1 tablespoon lemon juice
1/2 teaspoon salt
1 tablespoon chopped fresh parsley or 1 teaspoon dried parsley
1 teaspoon baking soda
1/3 cup unbleached all purpose flour
1/4 cup flour for coating
Tzatziki Sauce (see index)

Heat oil in a large frying pan on medium-low heat. Cook and stir the diced carrot, onion, garlic, cumin, 1/2 teaspoon salt, and pepper for 5 minutes or until the carrot is fork-tender.

In a food processor, pulse the garbanzo beans until they are broken into pea-size pieces. Add the tahini, lemon juice, and 1/2 teaspoon salt. Blend for 30-60 seconds or until the mixture is smooth. Dump the bean mixture into a large bowl and stir in the parsley, vegetables, baking soda, and 1/3 cup flour. Measure the remaining 1/4 cup flour into a flat dish. Form mixture into 12 patties, coat in flour and place on a greased baking sheet. Coat patties with cooking spray and bake for 20 minutes or until browned.

Serve on pita bread topped with Tzatziki Sauce (see index), lettuce, and tomatoes, or on top of a green salad with feta cheese.

Yield: 4-6 servings

TIP: *The flavor of dried herbs is much more concentrated than fresh herbs so you need to use less. As a general rule, use one-third the amount of dried herbs as you would fresh. When using dried herbs in a cooked dish, add them at the beginning so the flavor can incorporate into the dish. Add fresh herbs at the end so the heat doesn't destroy their flavor and color.*

VEGETABLE LASAGNA

Please don't be daunted by the long list of ingredients. There is no need to cook the noodles so this delicious, healthy, and hearty lasagna is simple to make. It is important to make sure that the noodles are completely covered by the sauce so they cook evenly. Use 6 cups of your choice of vegetables if you prefer them to those listed. Let the lasagna cool for 10 minutes before cutting to allow it to "set up" and hold its shape when cut.

Vegetable Layer:
Cooking spray or 2 teaspoons extra virgin olive oil
1 cup diced yellow onion (about 1 medium onion)
3 cloves of garlic, minced (1 tablespoon)
2 cups sliced mushrooms (about 10 whole mushrooms)
1 cup diced zucchini
1/2 cup green pepper, cut into 1/2-inch chunks
1/2 cup red bell pepper, cut into 1/2-inch chunks
1 cup chopped broccoli
2 teaspoons dried basil
2 teaspoons dried oregano
1 teaspoon salt
2 tablespoons grated Parmesan cheese
5-6 cups (40-48 ounces) store-bought organic pasta sauce or homemade Pasta Sauce (see index)

Cheese Layer:
1 cup frozen spinach, thawed, or 4 cups fresh spinach, cooked
2 cups (16-ounces) ricotta cheese (low-fat or regular)
1/2 cup low-fat sour cream
2 teaspoons dried basil or 2 tablespoons chopped fresh basil
1 teaspoon dried parsley or 1 tablespoon fresh chopped parsley
1/3 cup grated Parmesan cheese
1 egg or 2 egg whites
1/2 teaspoon salt
1/4 tsp black pepper
10-12 uncooked whole wheat or rice lasagna noodles
2-3 cups shredded mozzarella or Italian blend cheese
1/4-1/2 cup grated or shredded Parmesan cheese for top

Preheat oven to 350 degrees.

In a large skillet, heat the olive oil on medium heat. Cook the onions, garlic, and mushrooms for 3 minutes, then add the zucchini, bell peppers, broccoli, basil, oregano, and salt. Continue to cook for 5 minutes or until crisp-tender. Add the Parmesan cheese and 2 cups of the pasta sauce. Stir and remove from the heat.

Mix the ricotta, sour cream, basil, parsley, Parmesan, egg, salt, and pepper in a large bowl. Squeeze the spinach to remove as much liquid as possible then stir into the ricotta mixture.

In a glass 9 by 13 inch baking dish, spread 1-1/2 cups of pasta sauce. Place 3-4 uncooked noodles in the bottom of the dish (break the noodles to fit the pan). Spread the vegetable mixture on top of the noodles and smooth with a spatula. Add another layer of noodles, then another 1-1/2 cups of sauce. Spread the ricotta cheese mixture on top of the sauce then layer with more noodles and remaining sauce. Spread 2-3 cups of mozzarella cheese on top then sprinkle with Parmesan cheese.

Cover with nonstick aluminum foil and bake for 45 minutes. Remove the foil and bake uncovered for 10- 15 minutes or until the cheese is nicely browned and the noodles can be easily pierced with a butter knife. Let sit for 5-10 minutes before cutting and serving.

Yield. 8-10 servings

TIP: To squeeze the liquid out of spinach, place the spinach in a clean kitchen towel. Fold the towel over the spinach then twist ends in opposite directions to wring out liquid.

OVERSTUFFED BAKED POTATO

This recipe is great idea for a homemade meal when you aren't sure that you have anything in the house to eat for dinner. It is a favorite, easy to prepare meal in our family. I make it early in the day and set it in the fridge, covered with aluminum foil. Remove from the fridge 15 minutes before placing in a preheated oven and cook as below. My husband loves to slather his potato with hot sauce. I prefer plain low-fat yogurt or sour cream. This dish can be fully prepared then frozen in a sealed freezer-safe container for up to one month. To cook, let thaw completely then cook in a 375 degree oven for about 40-50 minutes or until the cheese is melted and golden brown, and the potato is heated through.

2 large or 4 small russet potatoes
2 teaspoons extra virgin olive oil
1 teaspoon minced garlic (1 clove)
2 cups mixed raw vegetables, cut into bite-size pieces (mushrooms, broccoli, onion, bell peppers, carrots)
1 teaspoon seasoning salt (for the veggie mixture)
1/8 teaspoon black pepper
1/2 cup cooked chicken or ham, cut into 1/2-inch pieces
2 tablespoons butter
3 tablespoons low-fat sour cream or plain yogurt
1/4 teaspoon salt
1/2 teaspoon seasoning salt (for seasoning the potato pulp)
1 teaspoon dried parsley
2 tablespoons milk
1/2 cup grated Parmesan cheese or shredded cheddar cheese
1 cup shredded mozzarella cheese

Preheat oven to 375 degrees.

Pierce potatoes and cook until fork-tender. To cook the potatoes, either bake in the oven for about 45 minutes or cook in the microwave for 10-15 minutes, turning over halfway through cooking. Set aside to cool slightly.

While the potatoes are cooking, pour the olive oil in a large skillet and set on medium-high heat. Cook the garlic and vegetables for a few minutes then stir in the basil, seasoning salt, and pepper. Cook for 5 minutes or until crisp-tender. Stir in the chicken and remove from heat.

While the potatoes are still warm, cut the skin off the top and discard (or save for another use). Using a tablespoon, scoop the flesh out of the potatoes into a large bowl. Leave a 1/2-inch of potato in the shell. Place the potato shells in an oven-safe dish. Mash the pulp with butter, sour cream, salt, seasoning salt, dried parsley, and milk until there are no lumps. Stir in the Parmesan cheese and vegetable mixture then scoop the potato mixture into the shells. They will be overflowing. Sprinkle mozzarella on top and bake for 35-45 minutes or until the cheese is melted and golden brown.

Yield: 2-4 servings

TIP: If you want to decrease the amount of carbohydrates in the above recipe, only use half of the potato once it is scooped out and increase the amount of vegetables. Save the remaining potato for another dish.

MEAT AND BEAN BURRITOS

To turn this recipe into Crispy Burritos, heat 2 teaspoons oil in a frying pan over medium-high heat. Lay the assembled burritos seam side down and cook for a few minutes on each side until brown and crispy. Top with sour cream and salsa.

1 pound ground turkey, buffalo, or lean beef
2 teaspoons extra virgin olive oil or grapeseed oil
1 cup chopped yellow onion (about 1 medium onion)
3 cloves garlic, minced (1 tablespoon)
1/2 green pepper, diced
1/2 teaspoon salt
1/2 teaspoon garlic salt
2 teaspoons chili powder
1 teaspoon dried oregano
1/2 teaspoon ground cumin
1 (15-ounce) can pinto beans, drained
1 (8-ounce) can diced green chilies, drained
1 (4-ounce) can tomato sauce
6 (10-inch) whole wheat flour or sprouted grain tortillas
Shredded cheddar cheese or Monterey Jack/sour cream/guacamole/salsa (for garnish)

Heat the oil in a large skillet on medium heat. Cook and stir the meat with a wooden spatula for 5 minutes, breaking it into small pieces. Add the onions, garlic, green pepper, salt, garlic salt, chili powder, oregano, and cumin and cook for a few minutes to brown the meat. Stir in the beans, green chilies, and tomato sauce, then simmer on low-medium heat for 10 minutes.

Place one tortilla in a dry hot skillet for 10 seconds on each side to warm and soften. Transfer to a flat surface and sprinkle some cheddar cheese on 1/3 of the tortilla. Place 1/4 cup of the meat mixture on top of the cheese then top with your favorite garnish (guacamole, salsa, sour cream). Roll up the tortilla, tucking in the sides as you roll. Repeat with remaining tortillas. Serve with a green salad.

Yield: 6 servings

REFRIED BEAN AND CHICKEN TOSTADAS

For a little variety, replace the chicken with 1 pound ground buffalo or lean beef, or use baby spinach instead of lettuce.

Chicken and Bean Filling:
2 teaspoons coconut oil or grapeseed oil
1/2 medium yellow onion, diced (about 1/2 cup)
2 garlic cloves, minced (2 teaspoons)
1 pound diced raw chicken breast or ground turkey
1 teaspoon ground cumin
1 teaspoon dried oregano
1/2 teaspoon crushed red chilies (optional)
1 tablespoon chili powder
1/2 teaspoon salt
3 tablespoons tomato sauce
1 (15-ounce) can refried beans (read the label to avoid hydrogenated fat)
1 (4-ounce) can diced green chilies, drained
Garnish: low fat sour cream, shredded cheddar or Monterey Jack cheese, lettuce, tomatoes, avocado, prepared guacamole.

Prepare Baked Tostadas (see below) and set aside.

Heat oil over medium-high heat. Cook and stir the onion, garlic, and chicken for 10 minutes; stir often. Add the cumin, oregano, red chilies, chili powder, salt, tomato sauce, refried beans, and green chilies and stir thoroughly. Reduce heat to medium-low and cook for 5 more minutes.

To serve, spread the tostada with the meat mixture and top with garnish, or serve meat and garnish in separate dishes and serve buffet style.

Yield: 6 servings (2 tostadas each)

Baked Tostadas

12 corn tortillas
4 tablespoons peanut oil, grapeseed oil or unrefined canola oil
Coarse salt for sprinkling

Preheat oven to 400 degrees.

Place 6 corn tortillas on an ungreased cookie sheet. Brush both sides of each tortilla with oil and sprinkle one side with salt. Bake for 6 minutes, flip the tortillas then bake for 4 minutes or until golden brown and crispy. Remove from the oven, transfer to a plate, and repeat with the remaining tortillas.

EGGPLANT PARMESAN CASSEROLE

The eggplant in this delicious, hearty casserole is baked instead of fried. My husband loves his eggplant thin and crispy. If you prefer it a little meatier, cut the slices 1/2-inch thick. Serve with extra warm pasta sauce on the side for pouring on top.

Eggplant Layer:
1 medium eggplant, peeled and sliced lengthwise into 1/4-inch slices
1/2 cup unbleached all purpose flour
1/2 teaspoon garlic salt
1/2 teaspoon salt
2 eggs or 1 egg and 2 egg whites
1/4 cup milk or water
1-1/2 cups whole wheat bread crumbs
1 teaspoon dried basil
1 teaspoon dried oregano
1 teaspoon salt
1/2 teaspoon garlic salt
2 tablespoons toasted wheat germ or flaxseed meal
1/4 cup Parmesan cheese
Cooking spray
3-4 cups organic pasta sauce or homemade Pasta Sauce (see index)

Cheese Layer:
1-1/2 cup low-fat ricotta cheese
1/2 cup low-fat sour cream
1 egg or 2 egg whites
1/4 cup Parmesan cheese
2 teaspoons dried basil
1/2 teaspoon dried parsley
1/2 teaspoon salt
1/8 teaspoon black pepper
2 cups shredded mozzarella and 1/4 cup grated or shredded Parmesan cheese for topping

Preheat the oven to 425 degrees.

Mix the flour, garlic salt, basil, oregano, parsley, and salt in a flat-bottomed dish. In a second dish, mix the eggs with the milk. Combine the bread crumbs, basil, oregano, salt, garlic salt, wheat germ, and 1/4 cup Parmesan cheese in a third dish.
Dip an eggplant slice into the flour mixture, then the egg mixture, then the bread crumbs, and set on a greased cookie sheet. Repeat with the remaining eggplant slices, arranging them in a single layer. You may need to use two cookie sheets. Spray the eggplant gener-

ously with cooking spray and bake for 15 minutes, flip, spray with cooking spray again, and continue to bake for 10-15 minutes or until brown and crispy. Remove eggplant from the oven and reduce heat to 350 degrees.

While the eggplant is cooking, mix the cheese layer. In a large bowl, combine the ricotta cheese, sour cream, egg, Parmesan cheese, basil, salt, and pepper; stir well to mix. Spread a small amount of sauce in the bottom of an 8 by 8 inch casserole dish. Arrange half of the eggplant slices on top of the sauce. Cover the eggplant with 1 cup sauce. Spread the cheese layer then add the remaining eggplant, overlapping slices to cover ricotta layer. Spread 2 cups of pasta sauce on top then sprinkle the mozzarella and Parmesan cheese.

Bake for 35 minutes or until the cheese is melted and golden brown (broil for the last few minutes to brown, if necessary). Let cool for 5 minutes before cutting. Serve with a big green salad!

Yield: 9 servings

For Zucchini Parmesan Casserole: Use 3 medium zucchini instead of eggplant, and follow recipe instructions.

For Eggplant Parmesan Sandwiches: Cook eggplant as instructed above, remove from the oven, top each piece with a few tablespoons of pasta sauce and mozzarella cheese. Arrange on a baking sheet in a single layer and broil in the oven for a few minutes until the cheese is melted and golden brown. Serve on toasted whole grain buns slathered with pasta sauce.

TIP: If you have trouble with the food sticking to the aluminum foil when covering dishes to bake, use nonstick aluminum foil or spray one side of the foil with cooking spray before covering the dish.

SWEET 'N' SOUR MEATBALLS

If you prefer to use the whole egg, double the amount of bread crumbs. For variety, replace the meatballs with bite size pieces of cooked chicken breast.

Meatballs:
1 pound lean ground turkey, beef, or buffalo
3 green onions, sliced
1 egg white or egg yolk
1/3 cup dry or fresh whole wheat bread crumbs
1 teaspoon minced garlic (1 clove)
1/2 teaspoon ground cinnamon
1/2 teaspoon seasoning salt
1/8 teaspoon freshly ground black pepper
2 tablespoons raisins, chopped finely
Cooking spray or 2 teaspoons coconut oil

Sweet 'n' Sour Sauce:
1 teaspoon coconut oil
1/2 cup thinly sliced carrots
1/2 cup red bell pepper, cut into 1-inch chunks
1/2 cup green bell pepper, cut into 1-inch chunks
1/2 (20-ounce) can pineapple tidbits with juice
1/4 cup apple cider vinegar
1/3 cup brown sugar
2 tablespoons arrowroot or cornstarch
1 cup cold water

Preheat oven to 350 degrees.

In a large bowl, mix the ground meat with the onions, egg, bread crumbs, garlic, cinnamon, seasoning salt, pepper, and raisins. With clean hands, combine the ingredients thoroughly. Form into 1-inch or 2-inch meatballs and set on a plate. Lightly coat a large frying pan with cooking spray and set over medium-high heat. Place the meatballs in the preheated pan, 1-inch apart. Cook for 6-8 minutes, turning to brown on all sides, then transfer to an 8 by 8 inch oven-safe dish. This may have to be done in 2 batches to cook all the meatballs. Add more oil or cooking spray if the meatballs begin to stick to the pan.

While the meatballs are cooking, prepare the sauce. In a saucepan, heat 1 teaspoon coconut oil over medium heat. Add carrots and cook for 5 minutes or until they begin to soften, adding more oil if needed. Add green and red bell peppers and cook for 2 minutes. Transfer to a bowl and set aside. Pour the pineapple juice, apple cider vinegar, and brown sugar into the saucepan and stir to dissolve sugar. In a separate bowl, mix the cornstarch with cold water until it dissolves. Add to the pineapple mixture and bring to a boil; stir constantly until it thickens. Return the carrots, red pepper, and green pepper to the saucepan and stir. Pour the sauce over the meatballs and bake for 25-30 minutes or until the meatballs are cooked through. Remove from the oven and serve meatballs and sauce over cooked brown rice.

Yield: 12 (2-inch) meatballs

TIP: When using very lean meat (ground turkey breast) to make meatballs or burgers, keep the meat moist by using the whole egg or the egg yolk instead of just the white and/or soak fresh breadcrumbs in milk before using.

MEATBALLS WITH KAMUT PASTA

Kamut pasta is a highly nutritious whole grain pasta without the heavy texture and taste of some other whole wheat pastas. Substitute your choice of whole grain pasta if you can't find Kamut. If your prefer to add a whole egg, double the amount of bread crumbs.

1 pound lean ground turkey, buffalo or beef
2 tablespoons finely diced yellow onion
1/2 teaspoon minced garlic
1 egg white or egg yolk
1/4 cup dry or fresh whole wheat bread crumbs
1 teaspoon seasoning salt
1/8 teaspoon freshly ground black pepper
1-1/2 tablespoons fresh parsley or 1-1/2 teaspoons dried parsley
1-1/2 teaspoons dried basil
1/2 teaspoon dried oregano
2 tablespoons grated Parmesan cheese
Cooking spray
2 cups Kamut pasta (or your choice)
2 cups (16-ounces) store-bought organic pasta sauce or homemade Pasta Sauce (see index)
Parmesan cheese for sprinkling

Preheat oven to 350 degrees.

In a large bowl, combine the meat, onion, garlic, egg, bread crumbs, seasoning salt, pepper, parsley, basil, oregano, and Parmesan cheese. With clean hands, mix the ingredients until they are thoroughly combined.

Form the mixture into 2-inch meatballs and set aside. Coat a frying pan with cooking spray and set on medium-high heat. Place the meatballs in the pan, 1-inch apart, and cook for 6-8 minutes; turning to brown on all sides. This may have to be done in 2 batches. Add more cooking spray if needed. Spread 1/2 cup pasta sauce in an 8 by 8 inch oven-safe dish. Place the meatballs on top, then add remaining sauce. Bake for 25-30 minutes or until the meatballs are cooked through.

While the meatballs are baking, cook the noodles in salted boiling water and lightly saute your favorite mixture of vegetables in extra virgin olive oil. Mix the vegetables with the cooked pasta; serve with extra pasta sauce and top with cooked meatballs. Sprinkle with Parmesan cheese.

Yield: 12 meatballs

TIP: *Make and cook extra meatballs then freeze in a single layer. Meatballs can be reheated from frozen. To reheat, pour pasta sauce on top and bake in a 350 degree oven for 30 minutes or until heated through.*

MEDITERRANEAN BURGERS

These burgers are delicious even without a bun. Serve with Sweet Potato Fries(see index) and a green salad.

1 teaspoon coconut oil or extra virgin olive oil
1/4 cup diced yellow onion
1/2 teaspoon minced garlic (1 small clove)
2 cups tightly packed fresh spinach or 1/2 cup cooked spinach, drained and chopped
1 pound lean ground buffalo meat, turkey, or beef
1/2 teaspoon Worcestershire sauce
1/2 teaspoon seasoning salt
1/8 teaspoon ground black pepper
1/2 teaspoon dried oregano
1 egg white
1/4 cup dry or fresh whole wheat bread crumbs
1/3 cup crumbled feta cheese

Preheat a grill to medium-high heat.

Heat the oil in a frying pan and set on medium-high heat. When the pan is hot, add the onion and garlic and cook for 5 minutes. Stir in the spinach and cook for a few minutes until all liquid has cooked off. Remove from the heat and set aside to let cool slightly.

While the spinach mixture is cooking, mix the meat, Worcestershire sauce, seasoning salt, pepper, and oregano in a large bowl. Mix well with clean hands to incorporate the seasonings. Add the egg white, bread crumbs, and spinach mixture, and mix well. Gently stir in the feta cheese gently so that small chunks remain.

Form into 4 large or 6 small patties. Cook on the preheated grill for 4-6 minutes per side then transfer to a plate.

Yield: 4 servings

TIP: If you have leftover crusts of bread or ends of buns, save them in a plastic bag in the freezer. When you have collected several, pulverize them in a food processor for about 15 seconds to make your own homemade bread crumbs.

PINEAPPLE BURGERS
WITH HONEY BARBEQUE SAUCE

If you are short on time, replace the homemade Honey Barbeque Sauce with your favorite store-bought barbeque sauce(with a few tablespoons of honey added).

1 pound lean ground buffalo, turkey, or beef
1/3 cup diced yellow onion (about 1/3 of a medium onion)
1/2 teaspoon garlic salt
1/2 teaspoon seasoning salt
1/2 teaspoon Worcestershire sauce
1/2 teaspoon minced garlic
1/2 cup canned pineapple, drained and finely chopped or crushed
Honey Barbeque Sauce (see below)

Prepare the Honey Barbeque sauce(see below) and let it simmer while you prepare and cook the burgers. Preheat a grill to medium-high heat.

In a large bowl, mix the meat, onion, garlic salt, seasoning salt, Worcestershire sauce, and minced garlic with clean hands. Add the pineapple and mix until thoroughly combined. Form into 4 large or 6 small patties. Cook on the preheated grill for 4-5 minutes per side.

Serve burgers with brown rice and salad or on a whole grain bun. The sauce can be served on the side or on top of burgers.

Yield: 4 servings

HONEY BARBEQUE SAUCE

Use this simple homemade barbeque sauce for Pineapple Burgers, as a dipping sauce, or to slather onto chicken or burgers while cooking.

1 teaspoon minced garlic (1 clove)
1/2 cup honey
1/4 cup white vinegar
1/2 cup ketchup or tomato sauce
2 tablespoons brown sugar
1 tablespoon prepared Dijon mustard
1 tablespoon Worcestershire sauce
1/4 teaspoon salt
1/2 teaspoon onion powder
Dash cayenne pepper

Combine the garlic, honey, vinegar, ketchup, brown sugar, mustard, Worcestershire sauce, salt, onion powder, and cayenne pepper in a small saucepan. Simmer on medium-low heat for 20 minutes or until the sauce has thickened. Serve with Pineapple Burgers. This will keep for about a week in a sealed container in the fridge.

Yield: 3/4 cup

TIP: *When cooking grains (rice, quinoa, millet) place a folded, clean dish towel between the lid and the pot to eliminate the typical messy splatter.*

VEGETABLES AND SIDE DISHES

TIP: A little oil goes a long way. When you are frying with oil in any recipe, start with the recommended amount. If the ingredients begin to stick to the pan, add more cooking spray or a few teaspoons of oil.

ZUCCHINI CHIPS

The bread crumbs, Parmesan cheese, seasoning salt, garlic salt, and pepper can be replaced with 1-1/2 cups Crispy Coating (see index) to speed up preparation time. Preheating the pan will help to crisp the chips but it is not a necessary step.

3 small zucchini, sliced in 1/4-inch thick rounds (3–4 cups)
1 cup unbleached all purpose flour
3/4 teaspoon salt
1/8 teaspoon black pepper
2 teaspoons Italian seasoning
2 eggs or 1 egg and 2 egg whites
1/4 cup water or milk
1 cup Panko or dry whole wheat bread crumbs
2 tablespoons ground cornmeal or crushed cornflake cereal
1/4 cup plus 1 tablespoon grated Parmesan cheese
1-1/2 teaspoons seasoning salt
1/4 teaspoon garlic salt
1–2 tablespoons coconut oil or grapeseed oil
Dash black pepper
2 teaspoons melted coconut oil or grapeseed oil
Cooking spray
Pasta sauce for dipping

Preheat oven to 425 degrees.

Mix the flour, salt, pepper, and Italian seasoning in a bowl. Lightly beat the eggs and water in a second bowl. Mix the bread crumbs, cornmeal, Parmesan, seasoning salt, garlic salt, and pepper in a third bowl. Coat the zucchini slices in the flour mixture, then egg mixture, then roll in bread crumbs until completely covered.

Brush oil onto a baking sheet and place in the preheated oven for a few minutes. Remove from the oven and arrange the zucchini slices on the preheated baking sheet in a single layer. Spray the slices generously with cooking spray. Bake for 7 minutes, turn chips over, spray with oil again then bake for another 5-6 minutes or until brown and crispy. Serve with warm pasta sauce for dipping.

Yield: 4 servings

For <u>Zucchini Fries</u>: Cut zucchini into 3-inch by 1/2-inch strips and proceed with recipe.

TIP: For crispy, coated vegetables, chicken, or seafood without deep frying: brush a baking sheet with a few teaspoons of grapeseed oil or melted coconut oil and preheat in a 450 degree oven before placing food on the pan. Bake at a high temperature (at least 425 degrees) until brown and crispy.

GRILLED ARTICHOKES

Cooking whole artichokes may seem intimidating but this recipe is simple and will impress your guests.

4 whole artichokes, stem cut to 2-inches
1/4 cup melted butter or ghee (clarified butter)
2 tablespoons extra virgin olive oil
1/2 teaspoon dried basil
1/4 teaspoon garlic salt
2 tablespoons grated Parmesan cheese

Cut off the top 2-inches of each artichoke and snip the ends of the leaves to remove the prickly parts.

In a medium pot, heat 3-inches of salted water on medium-high heat. Place the artichokes into the water, stems down, and reduce heat to medium-low. Steam until tender, about 20 minutes. Remove from the hot water, plunge into a bowl of ice water, drain the artichokes, and set aside. Preheat a grill to medium-high heat.

While the artichokes are steaming, mix the butter, olive oil, basil, and garlic salt. Slice the artichokes in half, lengthwise. Baste the flat side of each artichoke and set on the hot grill. Cook for 5 minutes, leaving charred grill marks. Remove from the grill, baste with butter mixture again, and sprinkle with Parmesan cheese. Serve hot with Basil Sauce (see index).

Yield: 6-8 servings

ROASTED ROSEMARY VEGETABLES

You can use any combination of your favorite vegetables for this recipe. Green beans, asparagus and halved brussel sprouts work well too!

1 cup cauliflower
1 cup (2 medium) carrots
1/2 cup yellow onion (about 1/2 medium onion)
1 cup broccoli
1/2 red pepper, seeds removed
1 teaspoon garlic salt
2 teaspoons crushed rosemary
1 teaspoon seasoning salt
1/4 teaspoon salt
1/8 teaspoon pepper
1 tablespoon extra virgin olive oil or grapeseed oil

Preheat oven to 425 degrees.

In a small bowl, mix the garlic salt, rosemary, seasoning salt, salt, and pepper. Cut the vegetables into bite-size pieces and place in a large bowl. While stirring, drizzle the vegetables with 1/2 tablespoon of olive oil and sprinkle with half of the seasoning. Drizzle the remaining oil, add the remaining seasoning, and stir well to coat evenly. Arrange the vegetables in a single layer on a greased cookie sheet and roast for 15-20 minutes or until crisp-tender and nicely browned.

Yield: 2-4 servings

TIP: Cauliflower is high in dietary fiber, Vitamin B6, and potassium.

PARMESAN BROCCOLI
AND CAULIFLOWER

2 cups broccoli, cut into bite-size pieces
2 cups cauliflower, cut into bite-size pieces
1 tablespoon extra virgin olive oil or grapeseed oil
1 tablespoon seasoning salt
2 tablespoons shredded or grated Parmesan cheese

Preheat oven to 425 degrees.

Place the broccoli and cauliflower in a large bowl. Pour half of the olive oil onto the vegetables then sprinkle with half of the seasoning, stirring to distribute evenly. Repeat with the remaining oil and seasonings. Arrange the vegetables in a single layer on a greased baking sheet. Bake for 8 minutes, remove from the oven, sprinkle cheese on top of the vegetables, and stir. Bake for another 6-8 minutes or until golden brown and crisp-tender.

Serves 2-3

TIP: Broccoli and asparagus are both good sources of protein.

ROASTED ASPARAGUS

This method works beautifully and tastes great with green beans or halved brussel sprouts too (even if you aren't a brussel sprout lover).

1 pound (16–20 spears) fresh asparagus
1–2 tablespoons extra virgin olive oil
Coarse salt and fresh ground black pepper for sprinkling

Preheat oven to 450 degrees.

Wash and break the ends off the asparagus. Arrange the asparagus in a single layer on a lightly greased baking sheet. Drizzle with olive oil then sprinkle with salt and pepper.

Roast for 5-8 minutes or until the asparagus is crisp-tender. Serve with Balsamic Reduction (see index)

Yield. 4 servings (6-8 spears each)

TIP: To break the ends off of asparagus, hold 2-inches from the the tip in one hand and the end of the stalk in the other. Bend asparagus away from you and the end will snap off, usually about 2-inches from the end. Discard the tough end pieces.

GARLIC BROCCOLI

Try this technique with green beans or asparagus as well. Vegetables can be refrigerated for up to two days after steaming. Remove from the fridge and cook vegetables in a skillet (as described below) before serving. Dunking the broccoli in cold water after steaming helps to retain a bright green color and crisp texture.

2 pounds broccoli, cut into bite-size pieces (about 4 cups)
1 tablespoon coconut oil or butter
2 garlic cloves, minced (2 teaspoons)
1 teaspoon fresh lemon juice
1/2 teaspoon dried tarragon or marjoram
3/4 teaspoon coarse salt
1/4 teaspoon black pepper

Fill a large saucepan with a few inches of lightly salted water and add the broccoli. Set on high heat to steam for a few minutes until crisp-tender. Dunk broccoli into a bowl of cold water for a few seconds then remove and drain well.

Melt butter or coconut oil in a large skillet over medium-high heat. Cook and stir garlic for 30 seconds, add the broccoli and cook for a few minutes, then toss to coat. Remove from the heat and stir in the lemon juice. Transfer to a serving dish and sprinkle with salt and pepper.

Yield: 8 servings

TIP: Use half butter and half coconut oil or grapeseed oil when frying foods on meduim-high to high heat. Butter will burn if used alone.

GRILLED VEGETABLES:

Use 6 cups of your favorite vegetables for this recipe. For an easy meal later in the week, cook extra vegetables to use in Grilled Vegetable Pasta Salad or Grilled Vegetable Soup(see index). If you don't have a grill pan, cut the vegetables in half lengthwise or into large strips, brush on oil and sprinkle with seasonings. Grill for 10-15 minutes or until tender then cut into bite-size pieces. To roast vegetables in the oven, arrange the vegetables on a greased baking sheet in a single layer. Roast in a 425 degree oven for 15-20 minutes or until tender and slightly charred. Grilled vegetables pair well with grilled chicken, fish, or burgers.

1 medium zucchini, cut into 1/2-inch rounds (1-1/2 cups)
3 large carrots, cut into 1/4-inch rounds (about 2 cups)
1 medium yellow or red onion, cut into chunks (about 1 cup)
1 cup cauliflower, cut into bite-size pieces
1 cup broccoli, cut into bite-size pieces
1/2 teaspoon garlic salt
1/2 teaspoon seasoning salt
1 teaspoon dried basil
1/2 teaspoon dried oregano
Cooking spray or 1 tablespoon extra virgin olive oil
Feta cheese crumbles for garnish (optional)

Preheat a grill to medium-high heat.

Mix the garlic salt, seasoning salt, basil, and oregano in a small bowl. Place all vegetables in a large bowl. Pour half of the oil on top or spray with cooking spray. Sprinkle half of seasoning and stir well to coat. Repeat with remaining oil and seasoning mixture. Cook the vegetables on a grill pan for about 15 minutes or until fork-tender and slightly charred, stir half way through cooking. Remove from the heat, transfer to a serving bowl, and top with feta cheese.

Yield: 4 servings

TIP: A grill pan is a metal pan with holes in the bottom, designed for the grill. You can use several layers of aluminum foil formed into a pan, or a pan without holes in it, instead of an actual grill pan.

PHYLLO SPINACH PIE

This dish has the flavors of Greek spanakopita but takes much less time to make. My family enjoys this dish served with warm pasta sauce.

8 sheets of whole wheat phyllo dough, thawed
1 teaspoon coconut oil or extra virgin olive oil
1/2 cup diced yellow onion (about 1/2 medium onion)
1 (10-ounce) package frozen spinach, thawed
1/2 cup cottage cheese
1 egg
1/2 teaspoon lemon juice
1/8 teaspoon nutmeg
1 teaspoon dried oregano
1/2 teaspoon salt
1/8 teaspoon black pepper
1 cup (4-ounces) feta cheese, crumbled
Cooking spray or 1/2 cup melted butter

Preheat the oven to 350 degrees. Spray an 8 by 8 inch glass oven-safe dish with cooking spray.

To squeeze the water out of the spinach, place it in a clean dish towel and twist ends in opposite directions to squeeze out water, or dump spinach into a colander and press with a spatula. Heat the oil in a frying pan over medium heat. Add the onion and cook for 2-3 minutes, stir in the spinach and cook for a few minutes more. Remove from the heat and transfer to a large bowl. Stir in the cottage cheese, egg, lemon juice, nutmeg, oregano, salt, and pepper, then stir to combine. Add feta cheese and combine gently.

Remove the phyllo dough from the box and unroll. Immediately cover with a clean, damp dish towel. Place 1 sheet of phyllo into the prepared dish, covering the bottom and sides. Spray lightly with cooking oil or coat with melted butter using a pastry brush. Place another sheet of phyllo dough on top. Repeat until there are 4 layers. Spread the spinach mixture on top of the layers of phyllo then cover the spinach mixture with another 4 sheets of phyllo dough, spraying oil in between the layers. Coat the top sheet of phyllo lightly with oil or butter.
Bake for 45 minutes or until the top is lightly browned. Remove from the oven and let cool for 5-10 minutes before cutting.

Yields: 6 servings

TIP: Phyllo dough dries out quickly when exposed to air. To use phyllo, remove one sheet at a time and keep the remaining sheets covered with a clean, slightly damp, kitchen towel.

STUFFED PORTOBELLO MUSHROOMS

Serve these mushrooms as a main dish with brown rice or quinoa on the side, or as a side dish with chicken or fish. This dish is also delicious with goat cheese or feta cheese added to the mixture instead of the Parmesan cheese.

4 large portobello mushrooms
2 teaspoons coconut oil or extra virgin olive oil
1/2 large yellow onion, diced (about 3/4 cup)
1 teaspoon minced garlic (1 clove)
1/2 small zucchini (about 1/2 cup)
1 cup chopped broccoli
1/2 teaspoon salt
1/8 teaspoon black pepper
3/4 teaspoon seasoning salt
1 teaspoon dried parsley
1 teaspoon dried basil
1/2 teaspoon dried oregano
3/4 cup frozen spinach, thawed and drained, or 3 cups
fresh baby spinach
1 teaspoon lemon juice
1 cup cottage cheese
1/4 cup Parmesan cheese
1-1/4 cups mozzarella cheese

Preheat the oven to 375 degrees. Clean the mushrooms and cut off stems. Dice the stems and set aside.

Sprinkle salt and pepper on the bottom side of the mushrooms and arrange, stem-side down, on a greased baking sheet. Cook for 10 minutes or until tender then remove from the oven.

Heat the oil in a large frying pan on medium heat. Cook and stir the onion, garlic, and mushroom stems for 5 minutes. Add the zucchini, broccoli, salt, pepper, seasoning salt, parsley, basil, and oregano, and cook for 3-4 minutes; stirring often. Stir in the spinach and cook for a few minutes or until it wilts. Stir in the lemon juice, remove from the heat and transfer to a large bowl. Add the cottage cheese, Parmesan cheese, and 1/4 cup mozzarella cheese to the vegetables and stir to combine.

Place the mushroom caps stem-side up on a greased, oven-safe dish. Spoon 1/2 cup of the vegetable mixture onto each mushroom and top with 1/4 cup mozzarella cheese. Bake for 25 minutes or until cheese has melted and is golden brown (broil for the last few minutes to brown the cheese).

Yield: 4-6 servings

TIP: To clean mushrooms, simply wipe off with a clean, damp towel. Running them under water can make them tough and rubbery.

STUFFED ZUCCHINI

This recipe is a good way to use up extra garden zucchini in the summer. Serve with grilled or baked chicken or fish.

3 medium zucchini
1–2 teaspoons coconut oil or extra virgin olive oil or cooking spray
1/3 cup diced yellow onion (about 1/3 medium onion)
2 cloves garlic, minced (2 teaspoons)
1 cup diced mushrooms
1 medium tomato, chopped
1 tablespoon dry whole wheat bread crumbs
1/2 teaspoon garlic salt
1 teaspoon dried basil
1 teaspoon dried oregano
1/4 teaspoon salt
1/8 teaspoon black pepper
3 tablespoons grated Parmesan cheese
1 cup shredded mozzarella

Preheat oven to 350 degrees.

Cut zucchini in half lengthwise. Scoop out the middle of the zucchini to 1/4-inch thickness; reserve the pulp. Lay the zucchini shells cut side up in a greased 9 by 13 inch oven safe baking dish and set aside. Coarsely chop the zucchini pulp and set aside.

Heat the oil in frying pan on medium heat. Cook and stir the onion and garlic for 3 minutes. Add the zucchini pulp and mushrooms; cook for another 5 minutes then remove from heat. Add the chopped tomato, bread crumbs, garlic salt, basil, oregano, salt, pepper, and Parmesan cheese and stir to mix.

Spoon mixture into the zucchini shells. Sprinkle each with mozzarella cheese, cover with aluminum foil, and bake for 20 minutes. Remove the foil and bake for another 5 minutes to brown the cheese.

Yield: 6 servings

SWEET POTATO AND APPLE CASSEROLE

This is a great side dish for Thanksgiving dinner. Assemble the dish in the morning and then before dinner, bake for 30 minutes, or until heated through and the potatoes are tender.

3 medium sweet potatoes, peeled and cut into 1/2-inch pieces
1/4 cup maple syrup
1/4 cup brown sugar
1/4 teaspoon stevia glycerite or increase brown sugar to 1/2 cup
1 teaspoon ground cinnamon
1/2 teaspoon salt
Dash black pepper
2 large apples, peeled and cut into 1/4-inch rings
1/2 cup raisins or dried cranberries

Preheat oven to 350 degrees.

Boil or steam the sweet potatoes for 15 minutes or until fork-tender. Drain, transfer to a large bowl, and set aside to cool.

In a saucepan, mix the maple syrup, brown sugar, stevia, cinnamon, salt, pepper, apples, and raisins. Cook on medium heat for 5 minutes, stirring gently, then remove from the heat. Pour the apple mixture over the sweet potatoes and gently mix. Pour into a greased 8 by 8 inch casserole dish and bake for 20 minutes.

Yield: 6 servings

HONEY MUSTARD GLAZED CARROTS

2 cups baby carrots, or carrots sliced into 1/2-inch rounds
2 tablespoons prepared Dijon mustard
1/4 cup agave nectar or honey
1/8 teaspoon lemon juice
1 teaspoon butter or coconut oil
1/4 teaspoon salt
Dash black pepper
2 teaspoons dried parsley or 2 tablespoons fresh chopped parsley

Pour 1 cup of water in a medium saucepan and set on medium-high heat. Place the carrots in the pan and steam for about 10-15 minutes or until fork tender.

While the carrots are cooking, mix the mustard, honey, lemon juice, butter, salt, and pepper in a small saucepan. Stir over low heat until the butter melts. Drain the cooked carrots and pour the sauce on top. Toss to coat, transfer to a serving bowl, then sprinkle with parsley.

Yield: 2-3 servings

PARMESAN BAKED FRENCH FRIES

1 cup Crispy Coating(see index)
4 cups red or golden potatoes, cut into 1/2-inch strips or chunks
2 tablespoons grapeseed oil or extra virgin olive oil
1-2 tablespoons Parmesan cheese

Preheat oven to 425 degrees.

Place the potatoes in a large bowl and stir in 1 tablespoon olive oil. Sprinkle with 1/2 cup Crispy Coating and stir to coat evenly. Repeat with the remaining oil and coating. Brush a few teaspoons of oil onto a baking sheet and place in the oven for a few minutes to heat. Arrange the potatoes in a single layer on the preheated greased baking sheet. Bake for 30 minutes, sprinkle with Parmesan cheese, then cook for 10-15 more minutes or until brown and crispy. Turn potatoes every 15 minutes for even cooking.

Yield: 2-4 servings

TIP: *It doesn't take much oil to coat vegetables for roasting. 1-2 tablespoons of oil will lightly coat 8 cups of vegetables enough for seasonings to stick.*

SWEET POTATO FRIES

Sweet potatoes are high in fiber and Vitamin A, Vitamin C and B6. With a naturally sweet taste, kids love them.

2 medium sweet potatoes (about 8 cups), cut into 1-inch strips or chunks
Cooking spray or 2 tablespoons grapeseed oil or extra virgin olive oil
1 teaspoon seasoning salt
1 teaspoon dried marjoram or basil
1/2 teaspoon garlic salt
1/4 teaspoon ground cinnamon

Preheat oven to 425 degrees.

Place potatoes in a large bowl. In a small bowl, combine the seasoning salt, marjoram, garlic salt, and cinnamon. Pour 1 tablespoon oil on top of the potatoes and stir to coat. Sprinkle with half of the seasoning mixture and stir. Repeat with the remaining oil and seasonings. Stir to make sure all the potatoes are coated well. Arrange potatoes in a single layer on a greased baking sheet and bake for 40 minutes or until brown and crispy. Turn every 15 minutes to cook evenly.

Yield: 4-6 servings

MIXED POTATO CHUNKS

This roasted mixture of white potatoes and sweet potatoes is a delicious and simple side dish for burgers, chicken, and fish. Keeping the skin on increases the fiber of the dish. It may seem like a small amount of oil to cover 6 cups of potatoes but it doesn't take very much to get the seasonings to stick.

3 cups red or golden potatoes, cut into 1-1/2 inch chunks
3 cups sweet potatoes, cut into 1-1/2-inch chunks
Cooking spray or 1-2 tablespoons extra virgin olive oil or grapeseed oil
2 teaspoons seasoning salt
1/2 teaspoon garlic salt
1/2 teaspoon paprika
1/2 teaspoon dried parsley
1 teaspoon minced garlic (1 medium clove)

Preheat oven to 425 degrees.

Clean the red and sweet potatoes with a vegetable brush but do not peel; cut out dark spots if necessary. Place the potato chunks in a large bowl. Mix the seasoning salt, garlic salt, paprika, and parsley in a small bowl. Drizzle potatoes with half of the olive oil then sprinkle with half of seasoning mixture; stir to coat. Repeat with the remaining oil and seasonings then stir in the minced garlic. Brush a baking sheet with a few tablespoons of oil and place in the oven for a few minutes to heat, then remove. Arrange the potatoes in a single layer on the preheated baking sheet and bake for about 40 minutes or until fork-tender and crispy brown; flip potatoes after 15 and 30 minutes.

Yield: 4-6 servings

For <u>Parmesan Potato Chunks:</u> Replace the sweet potatoes with 6 cups of red or yellow potatoes. Follow the recipe instructions. After 30 minutes of cooking, remove the pan from the oven and sprinkle 3 tablespoons of Parmesan cheese on top. Return the pan to the oven for another 15 minutes or until potatoes are fork tender and crispy brown.

VEGETABLE QUINOA PILAF

For variety, the quinoa can be replaced with brown rice, couscous, or millet (check the package of the grain for different cooking times).

1/2 cup quinoa
1 cup water or broth (vegetable or chicken broth)
Cooking spray or 1 teaspoon coconut oil
1 cup chopped yellow onion (1 medium onion)
3 garlic cloves, minced (about 1 tablespoon)
1 teaspoon ground cumin
1 teaspoon chili powder
2 cups diced zucchini
1/2 cup diced red or green bell pepper
4 cups packed fresh baby spinach or 1 cup cooked and drained spinach
1 teaspoon dried basil or 1 tablespoon fresh basil
1 tablespoon soy sauce or tamari
1 teaspoon lemon juice
1/4 teaspoon salt
1/8 teaspoon black pepper
1-1/2 tablespoons toasted pine nuts

To toast the pine nuts, spread them in a single layer in a dry skillet and set heat on medium. Cook for 3 to 5 minutes or until fragrant and lightly browned; stir often. Remove from the heat and transfer to a bowl.

Place the quinoa in a fine strainer and rinse. Shake the strainer to remove as much water as possible, and remove any debris. Toast the quinoa in a dry skillet until golden brown; stir often.

Bring the broth to a boil in a medium saucepan. Add the quinoa and simmer for 15-20 minutes until tender and all the liquid is absorbed. When the quinoa is cooked, transfer to a large bowl, fluff with a fork, and set aside. While the quinoa is cooking, heat the oil over medium heat in the skillet. Cook and stir the onion and garlic for 5 minutes, adding more oil if needed. Add the cumin, chili powder, zucchini, and bell pepper, then cook for 4 more minutes. Add the spinach and basil (if using fresh basil, add at the end when stirring in the lemon juice) and cook until the spinach is wilted. Stir in the soy sauce and remove from the heat.

Stir the vegetable mixture into the quinoa. Add the lemon juice, salt, and pepper; stir well and adjust the seasonings to taste. Top with pine nuts and serve.

Yield: 4 servings

For <u>Black Bean Quinoa Pilaf:</u> add 1 (15-ounce) can of drained and rinsed black beans to the veggie mixture after adding the soy sauce. Stir the bean and veggie mixture into the quinoa and continue with above recipe instructions.

SOUPS AND STEWS

CHAPTER EIGHT

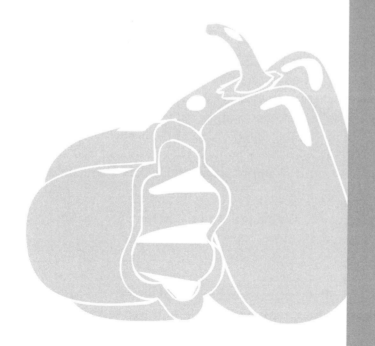

CREAMY TOMATO SOUP

This tomato soup has the healthy addition of several veggies blended in. My three boys love this soup and I love that they are eating a healthy serving of vegetables. If you have an immersion blender, you can use it to puree the soup right in the pot. Make a big batch and freeze extras in freezer-safe containers.

Coconut oil or extra virgin olive oil
1/2 large yellow onion, diced (about 3/4 cup)
1/2 cup diced celery (1-2 stalks)
1/2 red bell pepper, cut into 1/2-inch pieces
1/2 cup chopped carrots
1/2 cup diced zucchini
2 teaspoons minced garlic (2 cloves)
2 teaspoons dried basil
1/4 teaspoon celery salt
1/2 teaspoon anise seed (optional)
2 teaspoons salt
1/2 teaspoon ground black pepper
4 cups (32-ounces) no MSG chicken broth
1 (28-ounce) can tomato puree
1 (14-ounce) can diced tomatoes or 4 fresh tomatoes, chopped
2 tablespoons evaporated cane sugar
1/8 teaspoon liquid stevia glycerite or increase sugar to 1/4 cup
1 cup milk

Measure 2 teaspoons of oil into a large soup pot and set on medium-low heat. Cook and stir the onion, celery, red bell pepper, carrots, and zucchini for 3 minutes. Add the minced garlic, basil, celery salt, anise seed, salt, and pepper, then stir. Cook for 5 minutes, then stir in the broth, tomato puree, diced tomatoes, sugar and stevia. Cook on low heat for 15-20 minutes or until the vegetables are tender.

Using a blender, puree soup 2-3 cups at a time until smooth. If you prefer a chunky soup, set some of the vegetables aside before blending the soup. Return the vegetables to the pot, add milk and heat through, but do not boil.

Yield: 10 cups

SPICY TOMATO CABBAGE SOUP

This is a filling, low-calorie soup that is quick and easy to prepare. This soup freezes well.

2 teaspoons coconut oil or extra virgin olive oil
1 large onion, diced (about 3/4 cup)
1 teaspoon minced garlic (1 clove)
1 teaspoon dried basil
1 (32-ounce) bottle spicy vegetable juice
1 (14-1/2 ounce) can diced tomatoes
1 (12-ounce) can tomato sauce
1/4 head green cabbage, cut into 1-inch pieces
2 large carrots, cut into 1/4-inch rounds
1 cup green beans, ends trimmed and cut into 1-inch pieces
1 teaspoon salt
1/4 teaspoon ground black pepper
1 tablespoon evaporated cane sugar

Heat the oil in a large soup pot on medium heat. Cook and stir the onion and garlic for 5 minutes, then add the basil, vegetable juice, tomatoes, tomato sauce, cabbage, carrots, green beans, salt, pepper, and sugar. Stir well then reduce the heat to medium-low. Cook for 30 minutes or until the vegetables are tender.

Yield: 8-9 cups

For <u>Creamy Cabbage Soup:</u> Stir in 2 cups of milk after the vegetables are cooked. Heat through, but do not let the soup boil.

GRILLED VEGETABLE SOUP

This recipe is quick and easy when using leftover grilled vegetables. Prepare the grilled vegetables and refrigerate up to two days before. The vegetables can be roasted instead of grilled. To roast, preheat oven to 425 degrees, arrange the seasoned vegetables on a greased baking sheet and cook for 15 minutes or until crisp-tender and slightly charred.

Grilled Vegetables:
1 medium zucchini, cut into 1/2-inch half circles
3 large carrots, cut into 1/4-inch rounds (about 2 cups)
1 large onion, cut into large pieces (about 1-1/2 cups)
1 cup cauliflower, cut into bite-size pieces
1 cup broccoli, cut into bite-size pieces
1 tablespoon extra virgin olive oil
1/2 teaspoon garlic salt
1/2 teaspoon seasoning salt
1 teaspoon dried basil
1 teaspoon dried oregano

Soup:
3 cups chicken broth
1 (14-1/2-ounce) can diced tomatoes
1 (12-ounce) can tomato sauce
1 teaspoon salt
1/2 teaspoon ground black pepper
2 teaspoons evaporated cane sugar
1 teaspoon dried oregano
1 teaspoon dried basil
1/4 teaspoon cumin
1 cup cooked couscous
1 tablespoon dried parsley or 2 tablespoons chopped fresh parsley

Preheat a grill to medium-high heat.

Prepare the grilled vegetables. Mix the zucchini, carrots, onion, cauliflower, and broccoli in a large bowl. Pour the oil on top then sprinkle with the garlic salt, seasoning salt, basil, and oregano while stirring. Pour the vegetables onto a greased grill pan and cook for 15-20 minutes or until they are crisp-tender and slightly charred; stir occasionally. Remove from the heat and set aside.

In a large soup pot, combine the broth, tomatoes, and tomato sauce on medium heat. Stir in the salt, pepper, sugar, oregano, basil, and cumin. Cook for 10 minutes to heat thoroughly, stirring occasionally. Add the grilled vegetables and cook for 5 more minutes until heated through.

Ladle soup into bowls and top with warm cooked couscous. Sprinkle with parsley and serve.

Yield: 10 cups

CHICKEN CORN CHOWDER

This hearty soup pairs well with Zucchini Cheese Bread (see index) or crusty whole grain buns. I like to top this soup with Garlic Parsley Croutons(see index). Make a double batch and freeze the leftovers before adding the milk. To reheat, thaw the soup, add milk and heat through before serving. The chicken bouillon granules add flavor but aren't a necessity.

2 teaspoons coconut oil or extra virgin olive oil
1/2 large onion, diced (3/4 cup)
3 stalks celery, sliced into 1/4-inch pieces (1 cup)
6 cups chicken broth
2-3 golden or red potatoes, diced (1 cup)
2-1/2 (15-ounce) cans drained corn niblets or 5 cups frozen corn
1/2 red bell pepper, diced
1/4 cup arrowroot or non-GMO cornstarch (or more for thicker)
1 teaspoon no MSG chicken bouillon granules(optional)
1 teaspoon salt
1/4 teaspoon ground black pepper
1 large cooked boneless skinless chicken breast, cut into 1/2-inch pieces or shredded (about 2 cups)
2 slices nitrate-free turkey bacon, cooked and chopped
2 cups milk
Fresh parsley for garnish

Heat the oil in large soup pot on medium heat. Cook and stir the onion and celery for 3-4 minutes, but do not let them brown. Add 4 cups of chicken broth, the potatoes, corn niblets, and red bell pepper. Mix the chicken bouillon and arrowroot with the remaining 2 cups broth and stir well. Pour the mixture into the soup, season with salt and pepper, and cook on medium-low heat until the potato is fork-tender, approximately 20 minutes.

Puree half of the soup in a blender, or use an immersion blender, then return to the pot. This may need to be done in batches. Leave half of soup chunky for texture. Add the chicken, bacon, and milk, then heat through but do not boil. Adjust seasonings to your liking. Garnish with parsley before serving.

Yield: 16 cups

TIP: *To cut down on preparation time, use store bought rotisserie chicken when making soup.*

CHICKEN NOODLE SOUP

This easy to prepare soup is perfect when you are feeling under the weather. Make a big batch and freeze the leftovers. For really simple soup preparation, use 3 cups precooked chicken breasts or rotisserie chicken and add with the peas. To add more flavor to the broth, use 1 cup white wine and 2 cups broth to poach the chicken.

2 boneless skinless chicken breasts (about 1 pound)
2 teaspoons coconut oil or extra virgin olive oil
1 medium onion, diced
m10 cups chicken broth
1 tablespoon no MSG chicken bouillon granules
1 teaspoon dried sage
2 teaspoons dried thyme
2 teaspoons salt
1/2 teaspoon ground black pepper
2 cups sliced carrots (about 2 large carrots)
2 cups celery, cut in 1/2-inch pieces (4–5 stalks)
1 cup uncooked Kamut or whole grain pasta
1 cup green peas
1/4 cup cornstarch or arrowroot (optional)

In a large soup pot, add the oil and set on medium heat. Cook and stir the onion for 5 minutes, add 3 cups broth and bring to a boil. Add the chicken breasts, bouillon, sage, thyme, salt, and pepper, stir, and reduce the heat to medium-low. Let simmer for 20-30 minutes or until the chicken is cooked through. Remove the chicken from the liquid and transfer to a plate. Add the remaining broth, carrots, and celery to the pot and cook on medium heat for 20 minutes while the chicken is cooling.

When cooled for at least 20 minutes, shred the chicken with two forks, or chop into bite-size pieces. Add the pasta to the soup, bring to a boil, then reduce the heat to medium-low. Cook for 15 minutes then add the peas and chicken; let simmer for 5 minutes. To thicken, mix the cornstarch with 1/2 cup cold water. Stir into the soup with the peas and chicken and cook on medium heat for 5 minutes; stir often. Adjust the thickness of the soup by adding more cornstarch. Taste and adjust the seasonings to your liking.

Yield: 16 cups

For <u>Chicken Rice Soup:</u> Use 1/2 cup wild rice instead of pasta.

MISO SOUP

This healthful soup takes 10 minutes to prepare and is delicious on a cold day. Yellow and brown rice miso pastes are mellow and sweet and good for everyday use. If you prefer a stronger flavor, use red miso.

1/4 cup mild yellow or brown rice miso paste
4 cups water
4-ounces firm or extra-firm tofu, cut into 1/2-inch squares
1/2 cup oyster mushrooms, halved
1/2 cup shiitake mushrooms, halved
1/2 cup snow peas, cut in half
1/4 cup soy sauce or tamari
1-2 cups packed fresh baby spinach
1 green onion, sliced into 1/4-inch pieces

In a small bowl, mix 1 cup water the miso paste until smooth. Pour into a large soup pot, add the remaining water and set on medium heat. Stir in the tofu, mushrooms, and snow peas and let simmer for 5 minutes. Stir in the spinach and soy sauce and cook for 2 minutes or until the spinach is wilted.

Pour into soup bowls and garnish with green onion.

Yield: 6 cups

For Miso Noodle Soup: Increase miso by 1 tablespoon and water by 1 cup. Place 1/2 cup of thin rice noodles in a large bowl. Pour hot water over top until the noodles are covered. Let sit for 10 minutes or until the noodles are soft. Drain, then add to the soup with the spinach.

TIP: Dehydrated mushrooms are handy to have in a kitchen to add to soups and stews. Rehydrate mushrooms by soaking them in warm water for 10 minutes. Rinse thoroughly before adding to soup.

CHICKEN LENTIL SOUP

This thick soup is hearty enough to be a meal. Serve with a whole grain bun for dipping. Freeze leftovers for a quick healthy meal.

2 teaspoons coconut oil or extra virgin olive oil
2 cups sliced carrots
1 cup sliced celery (about 3 stalks)
1/4 cup diced yellow onion (about 1/4 medium onion)
1 cup diced zucchini
3 quarts (12 cups) chicken or vegetable broth
1 teaspoon dried thyme
1 teaspoon dried savory
1 teaspoon dried tarragon
1/2 teaspoon ground sage
2 teaspoons salt
1/2 teaspoon ground black pepper
1–1/2 cup dried green or brown lentils
1 cup white wine
2 cups cooked chicken breast, cut into bite-size pieces

Heat the oil in a large soup pot over medium heat. Cook and stir the carrots, celery, onion, and zucchini for 5 minutes then add the broth, thyme, savory, tarragon, sage, salt, pepper, lentils and wine. Cover with a lid and let simmer for 30 minutes.

Remove 4 cups of soup and puree in a blender or use an immersion blender for 15 seconds. Return the soup to pot, simmer for 15 minutes, then stir in the chicken. Cook for another 15 minutes or until the lentils are tender. Taste and adjust seasonings as desired.

Yield: 16 cups

MUSHROOM CHICKEN SOUP

For a more exotic taste, substitute 1-2 cups of the button mushrooms with rehydrated and chopped shiitake or oyster mushrooms (see tip on how to rehydrate mushrooms). If using precooked chicken, add it at the same time as the milk. Serve with whole grain bread or topped with Garlic Parsley Croutons(see index).

2 teaspoons coconut oil or extra virgin olive oil
1 teaspoon minced garlic (1 clove)
1 medium yellow onion, diced into 1/2-inch pieces
4 cups sliced button mushrooms
1 teaspoon dried thyme
1/4 teaspoon ground sage
1 teaspoon sea salt
1/4 teaspoon ground black pepper
8 cups chicken broth or mushroom broth
1/2 cup wild rice and brown rice mixtur.
1 boneless, skinless chicken breast, diced into 1/2-inch pieces or 1-1/2 cups cooked, diced chicken
2 cups fresh baby spinach or chopped kale
1 teaspoon dried parsley
2 cups milk (or increase broth by 2 cups)

Add the oil to a large soup pot and set on medium heat. Cook and stir the garlic, onion, and mushrooms for 5 minutes then add the thyme, sage, salt, and pepper; stir well. Add the broth, rice, and chicken and bring to a boil. Reduce the heat to medium-low and let simmer for 30-40 minutes until the rice is tender. Add the spinach, parsley, and milk and cook until the spinach is wilted. Taste and adjust the seasonings to your liking.

Yield: 14 cups

WHITE CHICKEN VEGETABLE CHILI

This recipe has the flavors of traditional white chicken chili but has the extra nutrition of several vegetables added. You control the amount of heat by adding hot or mild chile peppers or by adding hot sauce.

1 tablespoon coconut oil or extra virgin olive oil
1 large onion, diced (about 1-1/2 cups)
3 cloves garlic, minced (1 tablespoon)
3 cups organic chicken broth
1 teaspoon salt
2 boneless skinless chicken breasts (about 1 pound)
2 small zucchini, cut into 1-inch pieces (3-4 cups)
1 large red bell pepper, diced
1 large yellow bell pepper, diced
1/2 (15-ounce) can corn niblets, drained (or 1 cup frozen corn)
2 (4-ounce) cans diced green chilies
2 (15-ounce) cans cannellini beans, drained
2 teaspoons salt
1 tablespoon dried cilantro
1/4 cup finely ground cornmeal
Juice of 1 small lime

Heat the oil in a large soup pot and set over medium heat. Cook and stir the onion and garlic for 5 minutes then add the broth, 1 teaspoon salt, and chicken breasts. Cover with a lid, reduce heat to medium-low, and simmer for 15-20 minutes or until the chicken is cooked through. Remove the chicken from the broth and transfer to a plate; let cool.

Add the zucchini, red bell pepper, yellow pepper, corn, diced green chilies, one can of beans, 2 teaspoons salt, and cilantro to the broth and stir. Dump the other can of beans into a bowl and mash lightly, and shred or dice the cooked chicken. Add the mashed beans, chicken, and cornmeal to the vegetable mixture and let simmer on medium heat for about 10 minutes until the mixture starts to thicken slightly; stir often. Stir in the lime juice and remove from the heat. Taste and adjust seasonings. Serve with a dollop of low-fat yogurt or sour cream and sliced green onions for garnish.

Yield: about 10 cups

TIP: To shred cooked chicken, use two forks to pull the chicken apart. Hold one fork steady in the meat and use the other fork to pull. Shred a little for chunky pieces or a lot for finely shredded chicken.

MOROCCAN CHICKEN STEW

This stew tastes even better the next day when the spices have had several hours to intensify and blend together.

3 teaspoons coconut oil
3 garlic cloves, minced (about 3 teaspoons)
2 boneless skinless chicken breasts, cut into bite-size pieces
1-1/2 teaspoons salt
1/4 teaspoon freshly ground black pepper
1 medium onion, coarsely chopped
2 medium carrots, cut into 1-inch pieces (about 2 cups)
2 cups chicken broth
2 teaspoons paprika
1 teaspoon turmeric
2 teaspoons ground cumin
2 teaspoons ground cinnamon
1 teaspoon dried mint
1 (15-ounce) can chickpeas (garbanzo beans), drained
1/4 cup raisins
1/4 cup dried apricots, chopped (about 5)
1 (15-ounce) can diced tomatoes

In a large saucepan, melt 2 teaspoons of coconut oil on medium heat. Add the garlic and chicken, season with salt and pepper, and cook for 5 minutes or until the chicken has browned; stir often. Reduce heat to medium-low, and add one more teaspoon of coconut oil to the pan. Add the onion, carrots, broth, paprika, turmeric, cumin, cinnamon and mint; stir to mix. Stir in the garbanzo beans, raisins, apricots, and tomatoes. Cover and let simmer for 20-25 minutes until the carrots are tender. Remove from the heat and serve over warm, cooked couscous.

Yield: 4 - 6 servings

TIP: *Spice up plain cooked grains (couscous, quinoa, brown rice, millet) by adding your favorite lightly cooked vegetables and some herbs and seasonings (salt and pepper/parsley/ basil/curry powder/paprika/hot sauce etc...). Be creative and they will turn out delicious and different each time.*

SALADS

CHAPTER NINE

Grilled Vegetable Pasta Salad

BLT Pasta Salad

Chicken, Tomato and Basil Pasta Salad

Curry Veggie Pasta Salad

Three Bean Salad

Carrot, Broccoli and Raisin Salad

Baby Spinach and Strawberry Salad

Blue Cheese and Walnut Salad

Goat Cheese and Cranberry Salad

Green Bean Slaw

Jicama Coleslaw

Creamy Curry Coleslaw

Asian Salad with Glazed Pan-Fried Tofu

Cucumber and Watermelon Salad

GRILLED VEGETABLE PASTA SALAD

This salad can be served warm or cold and pairs well with chicken, fish or burgers. It can be made quickly and easily by cooking the veggies up to 2 days before. The vegetables can be grilled using a grill pan or layered aluminum foil. They can also be roasted in a 425 degree oven for 15 minutes or until crisp-tender and slightly charred.

Dressing:
1/4 cup low-fat mayonnaise
3 tablespoons extra virgin olive oil
1/4 cup orange juice
1/2 cup balsamic vinegar or white wine vinegar
1/2 teaspoon salt
1/8 teaspoon freshly ground black pepper

Salad:
1 medium zucchini, cut into 1/2-inch half circles
1 cup mushrooms, quartered
1/2 medium red onion, cut into 1/2-inch slices
1/2 cup sliced carrots
1/2 medium red bell pepper, cut into 1/2-inch pieces
2 tablespoons extra virgin olive oil
1 teaspoon garlic salt
1 teaspoon dried oregano
1 teaspoon dried basil
1 teaspoon seasoning salt or Nic's Mix(see index)
3 cups whole grain or Kamut spirals or penne
2 tablespoons chopped fresh basil
1 tablespoon fresh mint, chopped
1/2 cup crumbled feta cheese

Preheat a grill to medium-high heat.

Whisk the mayonnaise and olive oil in a medium bowl. Stir in the orange juice, vinegar, salt, and pepper, and set aside.

Place the zucchini, mushrooms, onion, carrots, and red pepper in a large bowl. Toss the vegetables with the olive oil then sprinkle with the garlic salt, oregano, basil, and seasoning salt while stirring. Grill the vegetables just until crisp-tender and slightly charred, 10-15 minutes; stir often. Remove from the heat, transfer to a bowl, and set aside.

While the vegetables are cooking, bring a large pot of salted water to a boil. Cook the noodles until tender but still firm. Drain the noodles and mix with the grilled vegetables, basil, and mint. Toss with just enough dressing to coat, then gently stir in the feta cheese. Save the remaining dressing in the fridge. The dressing will be absorbed by the salad overnight. Toss the salad with the remaining dressing before eating the leftovers the next day.

Yield: 6 servings

BLT PASTA SALAD

This filling, balanced salad is definitely hearty enough to be served as a meal.

1/2 head green leaf lettuce
1 cup cooked whole wheat or kamut penne or rotini pasta
1/2 cup shredded carrots
1/2 cup sliced cucumber
3 slices nitrate-free turkey bacon, cut into bite-size pieces
1/2 cup cooked chicken breast, cut into 1/2-inch cubes
1 large (about 1-1/2 cups) tomato, diced
1/3 cup blue cheese crumbles

In a large bowl, chop the lettuce then add the pasta, carrots, cucumber, bacon, and chicken; toss to mix. Top with the diced tomato and blue cheese.
 Serve with Honey Mustard Dressing or Balsamic Vinaigrette (see index).

Yield: 4 servings

CHICKEN, TOMATO, AND BASIL PASTA SALAD

To decrease preparation time, use a precooked chicken breast or rotisserie chicken. Squeezing the excess water out of the tomatoes helps to avoid watery pasta salad.

Salad:
1 boneless skinless chicken breast
1 tablespoon extra virgin olive oil or coconut oil
2 cups whole wheat or kamut pasta (shells, rotini or penne)
2 medium tomatoes
1/2 cup chopped fresh basil
1/4 cup grated Parmesan cheese

Dressing:
1/2 cup extra virgin olive oil
1 teaspoon salt
1/2 teaspoon black pepper
2 cloves minced garlic

Heat the oil in a skillet on medium heat. Cook the chicken breast for 6-8 minutes per side or until the chicken is cooked through. Transfer to a plate and set aside.

Fill a large pot with salted water and bring to a boil. Add the noodles and cook until tender but still firm. Do not overcook.

While the noodles are cooking, cut the chicken into bite-size pieces, chop the basil, and set both aside. Cut off the tops of the tomatoes and squeeze gently upside down over a sink or a bowl to reduce the excess liquid in the salad.

Prepare the dressing by whisking the olive oil, salt, and pepper in a bowl; stir in the minced garlic, and set aside. When the noodles are cooked, remove from the heat, drain, and pour into a large bowl. Add the tomatoes, basil, chicken, and Parmesan cheese, then stir to mix. Pour the dressing on top and stir to coat. Serve warm.

Yield: 3-4 servings

Variation: Serve a grilled chicken breast on the side instead of incorporating into salad.

TIP: When cooking pasta, add salt to the water to infuse flavor into the noodles. Cook noodles in plenty of water to allow them to swim. This will help to decrease the chance of them sticking together.

CURRY VEGGIE PASTA SALAD

Salad:
1 cup broccoli, cut into bite-size pieces
1 cup thinly sliced carrots
1 cup green peas, fresh or frozen and thawed
1/2 red bell pepper, cut into 1/2-inch pieces
1/2 cup green bell pepper, cut into 1/2-inch pieces
2 cups cooked whole wheat or kamut rotini pasta

Dressing:
2 tablespoons extra virgin olive oil
2 tablespoons agave nectar or honey
1/4 cup orange juice
1/4 cup red wine vinegar
1/4 cup plain low-fat yogurt
2 teaspoons curry powder
1 teaspoon dried thyme
1 teaspoon dried basil or 1 tablespoon chopped fresh basil
1 teaspoon garlic salt
Dash freshly ground black pepper

Fill a medium pot with a few inches of water and set on medium-high heat. Add the broccoli and carrots, and steam until for about 5 minutes or until crisp-tender. Do not overcook. Drain well and refrigerate to cool.

Whisk the olive oil, agave nectar, orange juice, red wine vinegar, yogurt, curry, thyme, basil, garlic salt, and black pepper in a bowl until thoroughly mixed; set aside.
Combine the peas, red bell pepper, green pepper, pasta, steamed broccoli, and carrots in a large bowl. Pour the dressing on top and toss gently to mix. Refrigerate for a few hours before serving.

Yield: 4 servings

THREE BEAN SALAD

This salad is high in protein and fiber, and low in fat.

Salad:
1 (14-ounce) can red kidney beans
1 (14-ounce) can white beans (navy or cannellini)
1 (14-ounce) can pinto beans
1/4 cup chopped fresh parsley
1/2 medium red onion, sliced into 1/4-inch half moons

Dressing:
2 tablespoons extra virgin olive oil
1/4 cup red wine vinegar
1 tablespoon minced garlic (3 cloves)
1 teaspoon dried basil or 1 tablespoon chopped fresh basil
2 teaspoons evaporated cane sugar or 1 tablespoon agave nectar
1/2 teaspoon salt
Dash black pepper

Combine the beans, parsley, and onion in a large bowl. In a small bowl, whisk the olive oil, vinegar, garlic, basil, sugar, salt, and pepper. Pour the dressing over the bean mixture and stir to coat. Refrigerate for at least 1 hour before serving.

Yield: 6 servings

CARROT, BROCCOLI AND RAISIN SALAD

This simple salad is an easy addition to a holiday meal. Prepare the salad and the dressing in separate bowls and set them in the refrigerator the day before the holiday meal. The morning of the feast, toss the salad and dressing together and refrigerate until dinner is ready. Top with Maple Pecans(see index) just before serving.

Salad:
2 cups broccoli, cut into bite-size pieces, lightly steamed and cooled
1 cup shredded carrots
1 cup sliced celery
1/2 cup raisins or dried cranberries
1/4 cup toasted pecans or Maple Pecans (see index)

Dressing:
1/2 cup low-fat mayonnaise
1/4 cup maple syrup
1/2 teaspoon celery salt
1/8 teaspoon ground pepper

Mix the broccoli, carrots, celery, and raisins in a large bowl. Whisk the mayonnaise and maple syrup together in a separate bowl then stir in the celery salt and pepper. Pour onto the salad and toss to coat. Refrigerate for at least 3 hours. Top with the pecans before serving.

Yield: 4 servings

TIP: To toast nuts, arrange nuts in a single layer on an ungreased cookie sheet. Bake in a preheated 350 degree oven for 8-10 minutes or until they become fragrant and golden brown. Check often while cooking as they will burn easily.

BABY SPINACH AND STRAWBERRY SALAD

This salad pairs well with grilled or baked chicken, fish or burgers.

1 (5-ounce) bag fresh baby spinach
1/2 cup red onion, thinly sliced and then halved
1/2 cup sliced mushrooms
1 cup fresh strawberries, sliced lengthwise into 1/4-inch slices
1/2 cup feta or blue cheese crumbles
1/4 cup sliced almonds or Maple Pecans (see index)

In a large bowl, combine the spinach, sliced onion, and mushrooms. Toss to mix then top with the strawberries, cheese, and almonds.

Serve with Honey Poppy Seed Dressing (see index).

Yield: 3-4 servings

BLUE CHEESE AND WALNUT SALAD

This salad is hearty enough to serve as a meal!

1/2 head green leaf lettuce, torn into bite-size pieces
2 cups spring mix lettuce
1/4 cup medium red onion, thinly sliced and then halved
1/2 cup carrot shreds
1/2 cup sliced cucumber
1/2 cup sliced celery
1 apple, cored and cut into bite-size pieces
1/4 cup toasted walnuts or Maple Walnuts (see index)
1 cooked chicken breast, sliced into 1/2-inch slices
1/2-1 cup blue cheese crumbles
1 avocado, cut into 1/2-inch cubes or slices

In a large bowl, combine the lettuce, onion, carrots, cucumber, celery, and apple. Toss to mix then arrange the sliced chicken, blue cheese, and avocado on top. Sprinkle with walnuts(see tip on how to toast nuts) before serving.

Serve with Balsamic Vinaigrette(see index).

Yield: 4-6 servings

GOAT CHEESE AND CRANBERRY SALAD

If you don't have time to fry the goat cheese rounds, simply crumble it on top of the salad.

Salad:
8 cups spring mix lettuce
1/2 cup thinly sliced red cabbage
1/2 cup carrot shreds or sliced carrots
1 cup sliced cucumber
1/4 cup dried cranberries
2 tablespoons pine nuts

Goat Cheese Rounds:
4-ounces goat cheese, cut into 1/2-inch rounds
1/2 cup bread crumbs or wheat germ
1/4 teaspoon garlic salt
1/2 teaspoon dried basil
1/2 teaspoon dried parsley
1 tablespoon coconut oil or olive oil

In a large bowl, combine the lettuce, cabbage, carrots, cucumber, cranberries, and pine nuts. Toss to mix and set aside.

Mix the bread crumbs, garlic salt, basil and parsley in a small bowl. Heat the oil in a small frying pan and set on high heat. Carefully dip the goat cheese rounds in the bread crumb mixture, coating both sides. Fry the goat cheese, about 15 seconds per side, until golden brown. Transfer to the top of the salad. Do not mix.

Serve with Balsamic Vinaigrette(see index).

Yield: 3-4 servings

GREEN BEAN SLAW

If you don't have the store-bought sauce for the dressing, feel free to substitute 1/2 teaspoon crushed red pepper flakes.

Dressing:
1/3 cup rice vinegar
1 teaspoon freshly grated ginger
2 tablespoons store-bought sweet red chili sauce or 1-2 teaspoons chili garlic sauce
1/4 teaspoon salt
3 tablespoons agave nectar or honey

Slaw:
1 cup green beans, ends trimmed
2 cups thinly sliced green cabbage
3 medium carrots, thinly sliced or cut into thin strips (about 2 cups)
1/2 cup red onion, thinly sliced
2 green onions, sliced in 1/2-inch pieces
1/2 cup red bell pepper, cut into 1/2-inch slices
1 tablespoon toasted sesame seeds or 2 tablespoons sliced almonds

Prepare the dressing; mix the vinegar, ginger, chili sauce, salt, and agave in a small bowl and set aside.

In a medium pot, boil 2-inches of water, add the green beans and steam for a few minutes until crisp-tender, stirring occasionally. Transfer the beans to a bowl of ice water for 10 seconds then drain well and place in a large bowl. Add the cabbage, carrots, red onion, green onions, and red bell pepper. Pour the dressing over the slaw and toss to mix. Refrigerate until ready to serve. Sprinkle with sesame seeds or almonds before serving.

Yield: 4-6 servings

JICAMA COLESLAW

Jicama is a sweet, crunchy vegetable that doesn't get soggy after being cut. It is is delicious in this light coleslaw.

Coleslaw:
1/2 medium jicama, shredded
1/2 green cabbage, cut into 1/4-inch thick slices
1/4 red cabbage, cut into 1/4-inch thick slices
1/2 daikon radish, peeled and cut into 1/4-inch half rounds
1/2 cup chopped watercress
1 cup diced red bell pepper

Dressing:
1 tablespoon extra virgin olive oil
1/4 cup fresh lime juice
1/4 cup agave nectar or honey
1/2 teaspoon salt
1/8 teaspoon black pepper

In a large bowl combine the jicama, green cabbage, red cabbage, daikon radish, watercress, and red bell pepper. Mix the olive oil, lime juice, agave, salt, and pepper in a small bowl. Pour the dressing on top of the slaw and stir to mix. Refrigerate for at least 30 minutes before serving.

Yield: 4-6 servings

CREAMY CURRY COLESLAW

The apple and raisins add a nice sweet flavor to balance the curry powder, but if you aren't a fan of curry, simply omit it. Leaving the peel on the apple adds fiber.

Dressing:
1/2 cup low-fat mayonnaise
2 teaspoons prepared Dijon or honey mustard
1 tablespoon agave nectar or 1 tablespoon evaporated cane sugar
1 tablespoon apple cider vinegar
2 tablespoons mil.
1/4 teaspoon curry powder

Coleslaw:
1/2 head green cabbage, shredded
1 cup shredded carrots
1 tablespoon celery seed
1/2 cup raisins or dried cranberries(optional)
1/2 cup diced apple, unpeeled
1/2 teaspoon salt
1/8 teaspoon black pepper

Whisk the mayonnaise, mustard, and agave together in a small bowl then stir in the vinegar, milk, and curry powder. Add more milk if the dressing is too thick to pour.
In a large bowl, mix the cabbage, carrots, celery seed, raisins, apple, salt, and pepper. Pour the dressing onto the coleslaw and mix well. Refrigerate for at least 30 minutes before serving. Serve with grilled or baked chicken, fish, or burgers.

Yield: 6 servings

ASIAN SALAD WITH GLAZED PAN-FRIED TOFU

This salad also goes well with sliced chicken breast instead of the pan-fried tofu.

Salad:
1/2 head chopped iceberg lettuce or Napa cabbage (about 3 cups)
3 cups spring mix lettuce
1/4 cup sliced celery
1 green onion, sliced into 1/2-inch pieces
1/2 cup shredded carrots
1/2 cup sliced red bell pepper
1/2 cup shelled edamame beans
Glazed Pan-Fried Tofu (see index)

Dressing:
1/4 cup brown rice vinegar
1/4 cup mirin(rice wine)
2 tablespoons toasted sesame oil
1/2 teaspoon salt
2 teaspoons minced garlic
1-2 teaspoons store-bought chili garlic sauce (for spicy) or 1-2 tablespoons sweet red chili sauce (for spicy sweet)
1/2 teaspoon freshly grated ginger
2-3 tablespoons honey or agave nectar

In a large bowl, layer the salad ingredients in the order listed. Mix the rice vinegar, mirin, sesame oil, salt, garlic, chili sauce, and ginger in a small bowl then whisk in the honey. Top salad with warm Glazed Pan-Fried Tofu(see index). Pour the dressing over the salad or serve the dressing on the side.

Yield: 4 servings

CUCUMBER AND WATERMELON SALAD

This light, refreshing salad is easy to prepare and goes well with grilled chicken or fish. Watermelon, cucumber, and feta cheese may seem like an odd combination, but it works!

Salad:
1 English cucumber
1/2 medium red onion, thinly sliced
2 tablespoons fresh chopped mint or 2 teaspoons dried mint
2 tablespoons chopped fresh parsley or 2 teaspoons dried parsley
1/4 teaspoon salt
Dash freshly ground black pepper
2 cups seedless watermelon, cut into bite-size cubes
1/4 cup crumbled feta cheese
Fresh parsley sprigs for garnish

Dressing:
3 tablespoons fresh lemon juice
1 tablespoon agave nectar or honey
3 tablespoons extra virgin olive oil
1/4 teaspoon salt
Dash freshly ground black pepper

Using a potato peeler, slice the cucumber into long strips and place in a large bowl. Add the red onion, mint, parsley, salt, and pepper and toss to mix. Add the watermelon and stir in gently; set the salad aside. In a small bowl whisk the lemon juice, agave, olive oil, salt, and pepper. Just before serving, gently toss the salad with the dressing and top with feta cheese and parsley.

Yield: 4 servings

TIP: An English cucumber is thin skinned and unwaxed so it does not need to be peeled. It has smaller seeds and is bred to be more easily digested than other varieties.

SALAD DRESSINGS

CHAPTER TEN

Xanthan gum is a thickener used in commercial salad dressings and ice creams and can be purchased in health food stores and online. I use it to give salad dressings a nice, thick consistency but it is optional in the recipes below. Dressings made with xanthan gum will thicken as they cool.

BALSAMIC VINAIGRETTE

This dressing has become a staple in our house. If you prefer your dressing less sweet, simply reduce the amount of agave or apple juice. If you are not using xanthan gum, simply mix all ingredients in a bowl or blender. Stir before serving.

1/2 cup (4-ounces) balsamic vinegar
1/2 cup (4-ounces) extra virgin olive oil
1/2 cup (4-ounces) unsweetened apple juice
2 tablespoons agave nectar, maple syrup, or evaporated cane sugar
1 teaspoon salt
Dash black pepper
1/4 teaspoon xanthan gum (optional)
2 teaspoons dried Italian seasoning (or 1 teaspoon dried basil and 1 teaspoon dried oregano or marjoram)

Measure the vinegar, olive oil, apple juice, agave, salt, pepper, and xanthan gum into a blender and mix for 10 seconds on high speed. Add the herbs and mix for a few more seconds then pour into a sealable glass container. Use immediately or refrigerate before serving. The dressing will thicken as it cools. Shake well before using.

Variation: Use red wine vinegar or raspberry vinegar instead of balsamic vinegar.

Yield: 1-1/2 cups

TIP: If you are not using xanthan gum, use half olive oil and half grapeseed oil to prevent the dressing from solidifying when refrigerated.

MISO SALAD DRESSING

2 tablespoons mild white or yellow miso paste
1/4 cup apple juice or orange juice
1/4 teaspoon freshly grated ginge.
1/2 cup brown rice vinegar
1/4 cup agave nectar or honey
1 tablespoon evaporated cane sugar or a few drops of stevia glycerite
1 green onion, sliced
1/8 teaspoon xanthan gum (optional)

Combine the miso, apple juice, ginger, vinegar, agave, sugar, onion, and xanthan gum in a blender. Process on high speed for 15 seconds or until smooth. Transfer to a sealable glass container and store in the fridge. Shake well before using.

Yield: 1 cup

CREAMY ITALIAN DRESSING

1/2 cup low-fat mayonnaise
1/3 cup white vinegar
1 tablespoon grapeseed oil or extra virgin olive oil
2 tablespoons agave nectar or honey
4 tablespoons grated Parmesan cheese
1 clove garlic, minced (1 teaspoon)
1/4 teaspoon garlic salt
1 tablespoon lemon juice
2 tablespoons evaporated cane sugar or 1/8 teaspoon stevia glycerite
1 teaspoon Italian seasoning
1/2 teaspoon parsley flakes

Measure the mayonnaise, vinegar, oil, agave, Parmesan, garlic, garlic salt, lemon juice, and sugar into a blender and process for 15 seconds on high speed. Add the Italian seasoning and parsley, then blend for 5 more seconds. Transfer to a sealable glass container and refrigerate until ready to use. Shake well before using.

Yield: 1 cup

HONEY MUSTARD DRESSING

This sweet and tangy, creamy dressing also works well as a dip, just mix in a few tablespoons of low-fat sour cream.

1/4 cup prepared yellow mustard
6 tablespoons honey or agave nectar
1/2 cup plain low-fat yogurt
4 teaspoons white wine vinegar or apple cider vinegar
3/4 teaspoon salt
2 teaspoons extra virgin olive oil

Measure the mustard, honey, yogurt, vinegar, and salt into a bowl and whisk vigorously until smooth. Stir in the olive oil, pour into a sealable glass container, and refrigerate until ready to use. Shake well before using.

Yield: about 1-1/4 cups

CARROT DRESSING

This dressing is similar to the carrot dressing served in Japanese restaurants. Gomasio is a mixture of sesame seeds ground with mineral rich sea salt. It is delicious on salads and vegetables.

1 medium carrot, cut into 1-inch chunks
2 tablespoons mirin (rice wine)
2 tablespoons brown rice vinegar
1 tablespoon soy sauce or tamari
1 teaspoon toasted sesame seed oil
1/2 small yellow onion, cut into 1-inch pieces
1 tablespoon grated or chopped fresh ginger

Combine the carrot, mirin, rice vinegar, soy sauce, sesame oil, onion, and ginger in a blender and puree for 30 seconds on high speed. Transfer to a sealable glass container and refrigerate until ready to use. Serve over chopped green leaf or iceberg lettuce and top with sliced green onions and toasted sesame seeds or Gomasio.

Yield: approximately 1 cup

HONEY POPPY SEED DRESSING

This creamy, low-fat, sweet and sour dressing is perfect with the Baby Spinach and Strawberry Salad(see index).

2 tablespoons white wine vinegar
2 tablespoons honey
2 tablespoons plain low–fat yogurt
1/2 teaspoon dry mustard
1/4 teaspoon salt
1/8 teaspoon freshly ground black pepper
2 tablespoons orange juice
1 teaspoon poppy seeds
2 tablespoons extra virgin olive oil

Pour the vinegar and honey into a small bowl. Whisk the mixture while adding the yogurt. Add the mustard, salt, pepper, orange juice, and poppy seeds then whisk in the oil. Transfer to a sealable glass container and refrigerate until ready to use. Shake well before using.

Yield: 3/4 cup

FRENCH TARRAGON DRESSING

3 tablespoons white wine vinegar
3 tablespoons apple cider vinegar
1 teaspoon Worcestershire sauce
1 small garlic clove (1/2 teaspoon minced garlic)
3 tablespoons honey or evaporated cane sugar
1/4 cup ketchup
2 teaspoons tomato paste
1/4 cup extra virgin olive oil
1/2 teaspoon salt
1 teaspoon dry mustard
1/8 teaspoon black pepper
1/4 cup water
1/4 cup apple juice
2 teaspoons dried tarragon

Combine both vinegars, the Worcestershire sauce, garlic, honey, ketchup, tomato paste, olive oil, salt, dry mustard, pepper, water and apple juice in a blender. Blend on high speed for 15 seconds, add tarragon and blend for 5 more seconds. Pour into a sealable glass container and refrigerate until ready to use. Shake well before using.

Yield:1-1/2 cups

COOKIES AND BARS

Chocolate Oat Jumbles

Oatmeal Chocolate Chip Cookies

Everyone's Favorite Chocolate
Chip Cookies

Oatmeal Raisin Cookies

Cinnamon Sugar Cookies

Gingerbread Cutout Cookies

Flourless Lemon Coconut Cookies

Peanut Butter and Honey Cookies

Fudgy Cocoa Cookies

Chewy Oat Cookies

Pumpkin Chocolate Chip Cookies

Chocolate Biscotti

Chocolate Chip and Almond Biscotti

Granola

Soft Granola Bars

Crunchy Granola Bars

Honey Oat Crackers

Apple Pie Bars

Date and Chocolate Chip Squares

Chocolate Topped Peanut Butter Cereal
Squares

Cereal Squares

Pumpkin Cheesecake Bars

Tip: One of my favorite tools for making cookies is a 2-inch cookie scoop. It is easy to use and results in uniform cookie size for even baking.

CHOCOLATE OAT JUMBLES

These not-too-sweet cookies are delicious and chewy when eaten thawed, or straight out of the freezer. If you prefer a sweeter cookie, add 1/4 cup more sugar. To intensify the flavor, use 1/4 cup Dutch process cocoa powder and 1/2 cup natural cocoa powder, or add 1 teaspoon espresso powder or Dandy Blend(see glossary).

6 large dates, stems and pits removed
3 tablespoons hot water or apple juice
3 tablespoons coconut oil or butter
1/2 cup plus 2 tablespoons honey or agave nectar
1 egg
1 teaspoon pure vanilla extract
1/4 cup brown sugar or 1/4 teaspoon stevia glycerite
1 cup rolled oats
1–1/2 cups quick oats
1/4 cup flaxseed meal or toasted wheat germ
1/4 cup powdered milk
3 tablespoons unsweetened shredded coconut
3/4 cup unsweetened cocoa powder
1/2 teaspoon salt

Preheat oven to 350 degrees.

Place the dates and water into a blender and pulse to chop. Add the coconut oil, honey, egg, vanilla, and brown sugar, and blend until smooth.
In a large bowl mix the rolled and quick oats, flaxseed meal, powdered milk, coconut, cocoa powder, and salt. Add the wet ingredients to the dry and stir well to combine. Drop spoonfuls of dough onto a greased cookie sheet and bake for 8 min. Do not over-bake. Let cool for 2 minutes on the pan then transfer to a cooling rack. Freeze extra cookies in a resealable plastic bag to keep fresh; thaw as needed.

Yield. 24 cookies

TIP: For the best results when baking or cooking in the oven, make sure that the oven has reached the desired temperature for at least 10 minutes before using.

OATMEAL CHOCOLATE CHIP COOKIES

2 cups quick oats
1/4 cup boiling water
1/2 cup butter or 1/2 cup coconut oil, softened
3/4 cup brown sugar
1/4 cup evaporated cane sugar
1/2 cup unsweetened applesauce
1 teaspoon pure vanilla extract
1-1/2 cups whole wheat pastry flour
1 teaspoon baking soda
1/2 teaspoon salt
1-1/2 cups chocolate chips or chocolate chip/raisin mixture

Preheat oven to 350 degrees. Measure oats and water into a bowl and set aside.
In a large bowl beat the butter, sugars, applesauce, and vanilla until creamy. In a separate bowl, measure the flour, baking soda, and salt, and stir thoroughly then mix in the chocolate chips. Stir the oatmeal into the butter mixture and combine with the dry ingredients. Stir well to mix.

Roll the dough into balls, place on an ungreased baking sheet and flatten slightly with a spatula. Bake for 10 minutes or until the bottoms are lightly browned. Let cool for a few minutes on the pan then transfer to a wire rack.

Yield: 36 cookies

TIP: *When baking cookies, take them out of the oven when the center is still soft and looks slightly underdone. Cookies will continue to cook on the sheet. Let sit for a few minutes then remove from the pan and transfer to a cooling rack.*

EVERYONE'S FAVORITE CHOCOLATE CHIP COOKIES

Of all the cookies I make, this seems to be the favorite of family and friends. They don't even notice the extra nutrition of the whole wheat pastry flour and wheat germ. If you are using whole wheat flour instead of whole wheat pastry flour, use only 1-1/4 cups of whole wheat flour and increase the amount of unbleached flour to 1-1/2 cups. I love the combination of chocolate, peanut butter and raisins but feel free to use 2 cups of chocolate chips if you prefer.

1/2 cup butter, softened
1/2 cup coconut oil or non-hydrogenated shortening, softened
3/4 cup brown sugar
3/4 cup evaporated cane sugar
2 eggs
1 teaspoon pure vanilla extract
2-1/4 cups whole wheat pastry flour
1/2 cup unbleached flour
2 tablespoons wheat germ or flaxseed meal
1 teaspoon baking soda
1/2 teaspoon salt
1/2 cup peanut butter chips
1/2 cup raisins
1 cup chocolate chips

Preheat oven to 375 degrees.

In a large bowl, whisk the butter, coconut oil, and sugars until creamy. Whisk in the eggs one at a time, then stir in the vanilla. Measure the flours, wheat germ, baking soda, salt, peanut butter chips, raisins, and chocolate chips on top of the wet ingredients. Stir until the wet and dry ingredients are well combined. The dough should be difficult to stir.

Drop spoonfuls of dough onto an ungreased cookie sheet. Bake for 8-10 minutes until the bottoms are lightly browned. The center of the cookie should look slightly underdone. Let cookies cool on the pan for a few minutes then transfer to a cooling rack.

Yield: 36 small cookies

TIP: For an easy way to have oven fresh cookies fast: Roll dough into 1-inch balls and freeze in a single layer on a baking sheet. When frozen, transfer to a resealable plastic bag. To bake, take out as many cookie balls as needed and place on an ungreased cookie sheet. Bake for 8-10 minutes at 350 degrees or until the bottoms are golden brown. Remove from the oven and let cool on cookie sheet for a few minutes then transfer to a wire rack. Frozen cookie dough will keep for up to 6 months in the freezer.

OATMEAL RAISIN COOKIES

These cookies are wholesome and delicious. For variety, substitute chocolate chips or dried cranberries for the raisins.

1/2 cup coconut oil or butter, softened
1/2 cup brown sugar
1/4 cup agave nectar of honey
1/2 teaspoon stevia glycerite or 1/2 cup evaporated cane sugar
1 teaspoon pure vanilla extract
1 egg
2 cups whole wheat pastry flour
2 cups rolled oats
1/2 teaspoon salt
1/2 teaspoon baking soda
1 cup raisins

Preheat oven to 350 degrees.

In a large bowl, whisk the oil and brown sugar until creamy. Add the agave, stevia, vanilla, and egg, and stir well. Add the flour, oats, salt, baking soda, and raisins to the wet mixture and stir to combine. Drop spoonfuls of dough onto a greased cookie sheet and bake for 8 to 10 minutes or until bottoms are lightly browned. Let cookies cool on the pan for a few minutes then transfer to a cooling rack.

Yield: 24 cookies

TIP: If your cookies are too thin when they bake, try one of the following: increase the flour by a few tablespoons, refrigerate the cookie dough for 30 minutes, add 2 tablespoons quick oats and refrigerate for 30 minutes, OR cool the pans (rinse with cold water then dry thoroughly) in between batches. These tips will help the dough to thicken, or cool the pan, to prevent the cookies from spreading too quickly.

CINNAMON SUGAR COOKIES

These snickerdoodle-like cookies melt in your mouth when warm.

5 tablespoons butter, softened
1/2 cup evaporated cane sugar
2 tablespoons low-fat sour cream
1 egg
1/3 cup honey
1/4 teaspoon stevia glycerite (or increase sugar to 3/4 cup)
1 teaspoon pure vanilla extract
1-1/2 cups unbleached flour
1 cup whole wheat pastry flour
1 teaspoon baking powder
1/2 teaspoon salt
3 tablespoons evaporated cane sugar
1 teaspoon cinnamon

Preheat oven to 350 degrees.

Whisk the butter and sugar together in a large bowl. Stir in the sour cream, egg, honey, stevia, and vanilla until smooth.

Combine the flours, baking powder, and salt in a separate bowl and stir to mix. Add the wet ingredients to the dry and stir well. Combine 3 tablespoons of sugar and 1 teaspoon of cinnamon in a small bowl and set aside. Roll the cookie dough into 1-inch balls, roll in the cinnamon sugar mixture and place on a greased cookie sheet. Flatten slightly with a fork or the palm of your hand. Bake for 6-8 minutes or until the bottom of the cookies are lightly browned. Remove from the oven, let cool on the pan for a few minutes then transfer to a cooling rack.

Yield: 36 cookies

For Iced Sugar Cookies: Follow the recipe with the exception of rolling dough in cinnamon and sugar mixture. Frost cooled cookies with Vanilla Frosting(see index).

For Lemon Sugar Cookies: Replace the vanilla extract with lemon extract and add 1/2 teaspoon freshly grated lemon peel. Eliminate the cinnamon and roll in sugar only.

GINGERBREAD CUTOUT COOKIES

Growing up, it was a tradition for each member of my family to decorate their own gingerbread man during the holiday season. I have carried on the tradition with my own family but came up with a healthier version of the original. For a crispier cookie replace the brown sugar with evaporated cane sugar.

1/4 cup butter or coconut oil, softened
3/4 cup brown sugar
1/2 teaspoon stevia glycerite or 1/2 cup evaporated cane sugar
1/2 cup unsweetened applesauce
1 egg
1/3 cup molasses
3 cups whole wheat pastry flour
1 teaspoon baking soda
2 teaspoons ground ginger
1 teaspoon cinnamon
1/2 teaspoon allspice
1/4 teaspoon ground cloves
1/2 teaspoon salt

Preheat oven to 350 degrees. Coat a baking sheet with cooking spray.

In a large bowl, whisk the butter, sugar, and stevia together then stir in the applesauce, egg, and molasses; mix well.

In a separate large bowl, mix the flour, baking soda, ginger, cinnamon, allspice, cloves, and salt. Add the wet mixture to the dry and stir well. Cover the bowl with plastic wrap and chill for 2 hours.

On a lightly floured surface, roll half of the dough to 1/4-inch thickness. Cut with cookie cutters into desired shapes then transfer to a greased cookie sheet. Repeat with the remaining dough. Bake for 10 minutes then let cool on the pan for a few minutes. Transfer to a wire rack to cool completely. Decorate with Vanilla Frosting(see index)

Yield: 20 gingerbread man cookies

TIP: To pipe icing onto cookies, scoop prepared frosting into a resealable plastic bag. Squeeze icing into a corner, twist the bag above the icing, then snip the very tip of the bag to create a small hole. Squeeze icing through the hole to decorate cookies.

FLOURLESS LEMON COCONUT COOKIES

These healthful, chewy cookies are delicious right out of the oven. Freeze extras and eat straight out of the freezer, or thaw before eating. Dried dates are high in fiber and iron and with a sweet sticky texture, they work well as a binder in cookies.

6 large dates, stems and pits removed
2 tablespoons warm water or apple juice
1/4 cup coconut oil or butter
1 egg
1 teaspoon lemon extract
1/4 teaspoon stevia glycerite or 1/4 cup brown sugar
1/2 cup agave nectar or honey
1-1/2 cups quick oats
3/4 cup rolled oats
1/2 cup high-fiber breakfast cereal
2 tablespoons toasted wheat germ or flaxseed meal
1/4 cup powdered milk
1/4 teaspoon salt
1/4 cup unsweetened shredded coconut
1 cup white chocolate chips
1 teaspoon freshly grated lemon peel

Preheat oven to 350 degrees. Coat a cookie sheet with cooking spray.

Place the dates, water, and coconut oil in a blender and pulse to chop dates. Add the egg, lemon extract, stevia, and agave, then puree until smooth.

In a large bowl combine the oats, cereal, wheat germ, powdered milk, salt, coconut, and white chocolate chips; stir to mix. Add the wet ingredients to the dry and stir well, then mix in the grated lemon peel. Drop spoonfuls of dough onto the prepared cookie sheet and bake for 10–12 minutes or until the bottoms are lightly browned. Remove from the oven, let cool on the pan for a few minutes then transfer to a wire rack.

Yield: 24 cookies

TIP: If the dough still looks wet, set the bowl in the refrigerator for 15 minutes to let the dough firm up before using.

For <u>Flourless Cranberry Spice Cookies:</u> Eliminate the coconut, lemon extract, and lemon peel and reduce the white chocolate chips to 1/2 cup. Increase the wheat germ to 1/4 cup, add 1 teaspoon pure vanilla extract, 1/2 teaspoon nutmeg, 1/2 teaspoon cinnamon, and 1/2 cup dried cranberries.

For <u>Flourless Chocolate Chip Cookies:</u> Eliminate the lemon extract, coconut, lemon peel, and white chocolate chips. Increase the wheat germ to 1/4 cup, add 1 teaspoon pure vanilla extract and 1 cup chocolate chips (or chocolate chip, peanut butter chip, and raisin mixture).

PEANUT BUTTER AND HONEY COOKIES

These cookies taste like a peanut butter and honey sandwich. Bake these cookies on the center rack in the oven to avoid overbaking the bottoms.

2 tablespoons butter or coconut oil, softened
1/2 cup non-hydrogenated, organic peanut butter
1/2 cup evaporated cane sugar
1/4 cup plus 2 tablespoons agave nectar, honey, or maple syrup
1 egg or 2 egg whites
1/4 cup unsweetened applesauce
1/4 teaspoon stevia glycerite or increase sugar to 3/4 cup
1 teaspoon pure vanilla extract
1-1/2 cups whole wheat pastry flour
1 cup quick oats
1/2 teaspoon salt
1/2 teaspoon baking soda
1/2 teaspoon baking powder
1 cup chocolate chips or raisins (or a mixture)

Preheat oven to 350 degrees. Coat a cookie sheet with cooking spray.

In a large bowl, whisk the butter and peanut butter together until smooth then stir in the sugar, agave, egg, applesauce, stevia, and vanilla. Whisk until smooth.

Mix the flour, oats, salt, baking soda, baking powder, and chocolate chips in a separate bowl. Add the dry mixture to the wet mixture and stir well to combine.

Scoop balls of dough onto the prepared cookie sheet and flatten slightly with a fork or spatula. Bake for 10 minutes until the bottoms are golden brown. Remove from the oven and let cool on the pan for 5 minutes then transfer to a wire rack to cool completely. Do not overbake. The tops of these cookies may look underdone but they will continue to cook on the pan after being removed from the oven.

Yield: 36 small cookies

TIP: *To avoid hard oil lumps in your dough when baking with coconut oil, try one of the following: whisk the oil with the sugar until creamy then add the other wet ingredients, mix it with warm liquid ingredients, OR mix it with liquid ingredients in a blender.*

FUDGY COCOA COOKIES

These dense, brownie-like cookies are delicious bites of chocolate. They keep best when frozen. Defrost by heating in the microwave for 15 seconds or put a few in a bowl and let sit out to thaw. To intensify the chocolate flavor, use both Dutch process cocoa and natural cocoa powders, or add 1 teaspoon instant powdered coffee replacement (see Dandy Blend in the glossary). The prunes and water can be replaced by 1/2 cup applesauce, or 1/2 cup pre-made prune puree.

1/4 cup prunes (5–6)
1/2 cup hot water
1/2 cup agave nectar or honey
1/4 teaspoon stevia glycerite (or increase sugar by 1/2 cup)
2 tablespoons butter, softened
1/4 plus 2 tablespoons brown sugar or evaporated cane sugar
1 egg
1/2 cup unsweetened applesauce
1 teaspoon pure vanilla extract
1-1/2 cups plus 2 tablespoons whole wheat pastry flour
1-3/4 cup quick oats
3/4 teaspoon baking soda
3/4 cup unsweetened cocoa powder
1/2 teaspoon salt
1 cup raisins
1/2 cup peanut butter chips or white chocolate chips

Preheat oven to 350 degrees.

Place the prunes and hot water in a blender and let sit for a few minutes. Pulse to chop the prunes, then add the agave, stevia, and blend for 15 seconds or until smooth. Whisk the butter in a large bowl then stir in the prune mixture. Add the sugar, egg, applesauce and vanilla and stir well.

Measure the flour, oats, baking soda, cocoa powder, salt, raisins and peanut butter chips on top of the wet ingredients and stir well to combine. Flatten slightly with a fork then bake for 7-8 minutes. Do not overbake. Remove from the oven and transfer to a wire rack to cool.

Yield: 36 small or 24 large cookies

For <u>White Chocolate Cherry Fudgy Cookies</u>: Replace raisins with 1/2 cup dried cherries and replace peanut butter chips with 1/2 cup white chocolate chips.

CHEWY OAT COOKIES

The secret ingredient in these cookies is apricot jam. It gives the cookies texture and flavor.

1/4 cup butter, softened
1/4 cup coconut oil, softened (or increase butter to 1/2 cup)
1/4 cup brown sugar
1/4 cup agave nectar or honey
1/4 teaspoon stevia glycerite (or increase brown sugar to 1/2 cup)
1 egg
1 egg white
1/2 cup fruit juice sweetened apricot or peach jam
2 cups rolled oats
1–1/4 cups whole wheat pastry flour
3/4 teaspoon salt
1 teaspoon baking soda
1–1/2 cups chocolate chips, white chocolate chips or raisins

Preheat oven to 375 degrees.

Whisk the butter, coconut oil, and brown sugar in a large bowl until creamy. Stir in the agave and stevia then add the egg, egg white, and jam; whisk vigorously.
In a separate bowl combine the oats, flour, salt, baking soda, and chocolate chips, and stir. Add the wet mixture to the dry and stir until combined.

Using a tablespoon, drop dough onto a greased cookie sheet. Bake for 8-10 minutes or until the bottoms are lightly browned. Let cool on the pan for a few minutes then transfer to a cooling rack. If the cookies spread too much while baking, add 1/4 cup more whole wheat pastry flour or refrigerate the dough for 15 minutes.

Yield: 36 cookies

TIP: Using brown sugar in cookies will result in a softer cookie. Using evaporated cane sugar will result in a crispier cookie.

PUMPKIN CHOCOLATE CHIP COOKIES

Every fall, I start to crave pumpkin sweets. These low-fat, moist cookies satisfy that craving.

3 tablespoons butter, softened
1/4 cup evaporated cane sugar
1/2 cup agave nectar or honey
3/4 cup canned pumpkin
1 egg
2 cups whole wheat flour
1 cup rolled oats
2 tablespoons wheat germ or flaxseed meal
1 teaspoon baking soda
1 teaspoon baking powder
1/2 teaspoon salt
1 teaspoon pumpkin pie spice
1 teaspoon cinnamon
1 cup chocolate chips

Preheat oven to 350 degrees.

Whisk the butter and sugar together in a large bowl. Add the agave, pumpkin, and egg, then whisk until smooth.

In a separate bowl, combine the flour, oats, wheat germ, baking soda, baking powder, salt, pumpkin pie spice, cinnamon, and chocolate chips; stir to mix. Add the wet ingredients to the dry and stir just until combined.

Scoop spoonfuls of dough onto a greased cookie sheet and bake for 10-12 minutes. Let the cookies rest on the pan for a few minutes then transfer to a cooling rack.

Yield: 24 cookies

TIP: Leavening agents have a shelf life of about 6 months. To test for freshness: place 1 teaspoon baking powder in a bowl and add 1/3 cup warm water and place 1/4 teaspoon baking soda into a bowl and add 2 teaspoons white vinegar. If the mixtures bubble, they are still active.

CHOCOLATE BISCOTTI

Biscotti are a classic Italian cookie. They are twice baked to be hard and crunchy--perfect for dipping in coffee, tea, or hot chocolate. There are several steps but they are actually simple to make and are worth the effort.

1-1/2 cup whole wheat pastry flour
1/2 cup quick oats
1/2 cup evaporated cane sugar
1/2 unsweetened cocoa powder
1/4 cup chocolate chips
1/4 cup white chocolate chips
1/2 teaspoon baking powder
1/2 teaspoon baking soda
1/2 teaspoon salt
1 teaspoon pure vanilla extract
2 eggs
1 egg white
1/2 teaspoon stevia glycerite (or increase sugar to 1 cup)

Preheat oven to 350 degrees.

Measure the flour, oats, sugar, cocoa powder, chocolate chips, white chocolate chips, baking powder, baking soda, and salt in a large bowl and stir.

In a separate bowl, mix the vanilla, eggs, egg white, and stevia and stir with a whisk. Add the wet ingredients to the dry and stir until combined. Divide the dough in half. With floured hands, shape the dough into 2 (8-inch) rolls, pat down to 1/2-inch thickness and place on a greased cookie sheet. Bake for 25 minutes, remove from the oven and reduce temperature to 325 degrees. Transfer the rolls to a wire rack and let cool for 10 minutes.

Cut each roll into 8 slices and return slices to the oven. Bake for an additional 6-8 minutes on each side. Remove from the oven and let cool completely on a wire rack. Store in airtight container for up to two weeks.

Yield: 16 biscotti

CHOCOLATE CHIP
AND ALMOND BISCOTTI

Oats, nuts, flaxseed, and wheat germ make this biscotti a nutrition-packed treat. They are crunchy and perfect for dunking in coffee, tea, or hot chocolate.

1–1/2 cups whole wheat pastry flour or whole wheat flour
3/4 cup evaporated cane sugar
1/2 cup quick oats
1/4 cup sliced almonds
2 tablespoons toasted wheat germ
2 tablespoons flaxseed meal
2 tablespoons baking powder
1/2 teaspoon salt
1/2 cup mini chocolate chips (or chopped chocolate chips)
1 tablespoon grapeseed oil or canola oil
2 eggs
1 egg white
2 teaspoons almond extract
1 teaspoon pure vanilla extract
1/4 teaspoon stevia glycerite (or increase sugar to 1 cup)

Preheat oven to 350 degrees.

Mix the flour, sugar, oats, almonds, wheat germ, flaxseed meal, baking powder, salt and chocolate chips in a large bowl.

In a separate bowl, stir the oil, eggs, egg white, almond and vanilla extracts, and stevia. Add the wet ingredients to the dry and stir well. The mixture will seem crumbly. Mix with clean hands until a ball can be formed. Divide the dough in half, shape into 2 (8-inch) rolls then flatten to 1-inch. Bake for 30 minutes, remove from the oven then reduce temperature to 325 degrees.

Let the rolls cool for 10 minutes then cut into 8-10 slices. Return slices to the oven and bake for an additional 8-10 minutes on each side. The slices should be lightly toasted. Remove from the oven and set on a wire rack to cool completely. Store in an airtight container for up to two weeks.

Yield. 18-20 biscotti

Chocolate Dipped Almond Biscotti: Follow recipe instructions but do not add the chocolate chips to the batter. After the biscotti have cooled, melt 1/2 cup of chocolate chips in a small pan over low heat. Dip the bottom (flat side) of each biscotti in the melted chocolate then lay upside down on a wire rack to cool.

GRANOLA

This granola will keep in an airtight container for about a month. Sprinkle on top of cereal, or on yogurt and fruit.

3 cups rolled oats
1/2 cup chopped almonds
2 tablespoons toasted wheat germ
2 tablespoon flaxseed meal or increase wheat germ to 1/4 cup
1/4 cup raw pumpkin seeds
2 tablespoons raw sunflower seeds
2 tablespoons powdered milk
2 tablespoons coconut oil
1/2 cup honey
2 tablespoons maple syrup
2 tablespoons brown rice syrup (or increase maple syrup to 1/4 cup)
1 teaspoon ground cinnamon
1/4 teaspoon salt
2 teaspoons pure vanilla extract
1 cup raisins
1/2 dried cranberries or dried blueberries

Preheat oven to 325 degrees. Line a cookie sheet with nonstick aluminum foil or coat foil with cooking spray.

Combine the oats, almonds, wheat germ, flaxseed meal, pumpkin seeds, sunflower seeds, and powdered milk in a large bowl and set aside.

In a small saucepan measure the coconut oil, honey, maple syrup, and brown rice syrup. Heat on low until the mixture liquefies, then stir in the cinnamon and salt. Remove from the heat and stir in the vanilla. Pour the wet mixture over the dry and stir well to coat the oat mixture. Spread onto the prepared cookie sheet. Bake for 15 minutes then flip granola pieces with a spatula. Return to the oven and flip every 5 minutes for a total of 30 minutes. Remove from the oven and stir in the dried fruit. Let cool completely then transfer to an airtight container.

Yield: 6 cups

SOFT GRANOLA BARS

These bars are healthy and filling. They are perfect for an on-the-go snack. Freeze extra bars in layers separated by wax paper. Remove from the freezer and thaw as needed.

10 large dates or 5 large dates and 5 prunes, pits and stems removed
1/2 cup warm apple juice or warm water
2 tablespoons coconut oil
1/2 cup plus 2 tablespoons honey or agave nectar
2 tablespoons brown rice syrup or organic corn syrup
1/2 teaspoon stevia glycerite or 1/2 cup brown sugar
2 cups rolled oats
1-1/2 cups quick oats
1 cup high-fiber breakfast cereal
2 tablespoons wheat germ
2 tablespoons flaxseed meal or ground nuts
1/2 cup powdered milk or protein powder
3/4 teaspoon salt
1 cup sliced or chopped raw almonds
1 cup mixture of your choice (raisins/dried apricots/chocolate chips, dried cherries, dried blueberries)

Preheat oven to 350 degrees. Grease a cookie sheet or a 9 by 13 inch oven-safe glass baking dish.

Place the dates in a blender, add the warm apple juice , let sit for a few minutes then pulse to chop the dates. Add the coconut oil, honey, brown rice syrup, and stevia, and puree until smooth.

In a large bowl, stir the rolled oats, quick oats, cereal, wheat germ, flaxseed meal, powdered milk, salt, nuts, and dried fruit. Add the wet ingredients to the dry and stir well to combine. The mixture should stick together; if it seems dry, add one tablespoon of honey.

Firmly press the mixture into the prepared pan and spread evenly. Bake on the center rack for 30 minutes or until the edges are brown. Remove from the oven, let cool for 10 minutes on a wire rack, then cut into bars. Let cool for another 20 minutes before carefully removing from the pan. These will keep for up to 2 weeks in an airtight container.

Yield: 20 bars

For Cherry White Chocolate Chip Granola Bars: Add 1/2 cup white chocolate chips and 1/2 cup dried cherries and eliminate the dried fruit mixture.

For Spiced Granola Bars: Add 1 teaspoon cinnamon, 1/4 teaspoon nutmeg and 1/8 teaspoon ground cloves or 1-1/2 teaspoons pumpkin pie spice to the batter before baking.

TIP: To press bars into the pan, spray a spatula with cooking spray to prevent sticking.

CRUNCHY GRANOLA BARS

These crispy and delicious granola bars are a great snack for kids and adults. Use a stone-ware cookie sheet if you have one.

1/2 cup honey
3 tablespoons brown rice syrup (or organic corn syrup)
2-1/2 tablespoons coconut oil or unsalted butter
1/4 cup brown sugar or evaporated cane sugar
1/2 teaspoon salt
2 teaspoons pure vanilla extract
2 cups rolled oats
1 cup high-fiber breakfast cereal
1/4 cup raw pumpkin seeds
1/4 cup raw sunflower seeds
1/2 cup sliced raw almonds
2 tablespoons wheat germ
1 tablespoon flaxseed meal (or increase wheat germ to 3 tablespoons)
2 tablespoons wheat bran
3 tablespoons powdered milk
1/2 teaspoon cinnamon
1-1/2 cups dried fruit mixture (raisins, dried cherries, dried cranberries, dried blueberries)

Preheat oven to 325 degrees. Grease a 9 by 13 oven safe baking dish.

Mix the honey, brown rice syrup, coconut oil, brown sugar, and salt in a small saucepan. Heat on low for 5 minutes or until the sugar is dissolved. Remove from the heat and stir in the vanilla.

In a separate bowl mix the oats, cereal, pumpkin seeds, sunflower seeds, almonds, wheat germ, flaxseed meal, wheat bran, powdered milk, cinnamon and dried fruit. Stir well to combine. Pour the liquid mixture onto the dry and stir well until the oat mixture is completely coated.

Firmly press the mixture into the prepared baking dish and bake for 25 minutes. Remove from the oven, let cool for 5 minutes then cut into squares. Bake for 15 minutes more. Remove from the oven, let cool for 15 minutes, then transfer bars to a wire rack to cool completely. Store in an airtight container for up to 2 weeks.

Yield: 20 bars

For Toasted Oat Granola Bars: Preheat the oven to 350 degrees. Toast the oats, wheat germ, sunflower seeds, and almonds on a dry cookie sheet for 15 minutes or until lightly browned; stirring every 5 minutes. Remove from the oven, let cool, then proceed with the recipe.

HONEY OAT CRACKERS

Kids love these lightly sweet crackers (and so do I). To make your own animal crackers, use animal shaped cookie cutters instead of cutting the dough into squares!

2 cups rolled oats
1 cup whole wheat pastry flour
1 tablespoon wheat germ or flaxseed meal
1/4 cup quick oats
1/4 teaspoon baking soda
1/2 teaspoon salt
1/4 cup evaporated cane sugar
5 tablespoons coconut oil or butter, softened
1/2 cup plus 2 tablespoons honey
2 tablespoons water

Preheat oven to 350 degrees.

Pour 2 cups rolled oats into a blender and pulverize until finely ground. Transfer to a large bowl and add the flour, wheat germ, quick oats, baking soda, salt, and sugar. Cut in the coconut oil using a pastry cutter or a fork. With a wooden spoon, mix in the honey, then add the water 1 tablespoon at a time. The dough may still seem dry. Mix with clean hands until a ball can be formed then divide the ball in half. If the dough is still too dry to form a ball, mix in one more tablespoon of honey before dividing.

Roll half of dough out on a lightly floured surface and cut into 2-inch squares. Transfer to a greased cookie sheet and bake for 10 minutes or until the edges begin to brown. Let cool on the pan for a few minutes then transfer to a wire rack. Let crackers cool completely then transfer to an airtight container. These will keep for up to 2 weeks.

Yield: 60 crackers

For <u>Cinnamon Sugar Crackers:</u> Mix 2 tablespoons evaporated cane sugar and 1/2 teaspoon cinnamon in a small bowl. Sprinkle onto the crackers before baking.

APPLE PIE BARS

If you are using coconut oil, make sure that the honey and apple juice are at room temperature or warm, to avoid hard coconut oil lumps. Serve with Sweet Yogurt cream (see index) or frozen non-dairy whipped topping.

1–1/2 cups whole wheat pastry flour
1 cup rolled oats
1 tablespoon toasted wheat germ
1/3 cup brown sugar
1/4 teaspoon stevia glycerite or 1/4 cup evaporated cane sugar
3/4 teaspoon baking powder
1/4 teaspoon salt
1/2 teaspoon cinnamon
1/4 teaspoon nutmeg
3 tablespoons coconut oil or butter, softened
1/2 cup plus 2 tablespoons brown sugar or room temperature agave nectar or honey
2 tablespoons apple juice, at room temperature
Dash salt
3 cups finely diced apples (peeled or unpeeled)

Preheat oven to 350 degrees. Lightly grease a 9 by 9 inch square baking dish.

Mix the flour, oats, wheat germ, brown sugar, stevia, baking powder, salt, cinnamon, and nutmeg in a large bowl.

In a separate bowl, whisk the coconut oil and 1/2 cup brown sugar or agave until smooth and creamy. Add the apple juice and stir to combine. Add the wet mixture to the dry and stir until the mixture resembles coarse crumbs. Press 1-1/2 cups loosely packed oat mixture into the bottom of the pan.

In a bowl, mix the diced apples with the remaining 2 tablespoons of brown sugar or agave, and a dash of salt. Spread evenly over the crust. Pour the remaining oat mixture on top and spread to cover the apples.

Bake for 30-35 minutes or until the top begins to brown and the apples are fork-tender. Remove from the oven the let cool for 15 minutes before cutting and serving.

Yield: 12 bars

For <u>Apple Berry or Apple Peach Bars:</u> Decrease apples to 1 cup and add 2 cups of your favorite fresh or thawed fruit (berries, peaches, etc...).

TIP: To soften hardened brown sugar, place a piece of bread or a slice of apple with the brown sugar in a sealed container. Remove bread or apple after 24 hours and discard.

DATE AND CHOCOLATE CHIP SQUARES

The fiber from the whole wheat pastry flour and oats, and iron from the dates give these bars a nutrition boost. The addition of chocolate chips makes these date squares extraordinary!

Filling:
1–1/4 cups water
2–1/2 cups large dates, stems and pits removed
1/2 teaspoon salt
1/8 teaspoon stevia glycerite or 2 tablespoons agave nectar or honey
1 cup chocolate chips

Crust:
3–1/2 cups rolled oats
2 cups whole wheat pastry flour
2 tablespoons wheat germ or flaxseed meal
1/2 cup brown sugar
1/2 teaspoon salt
1/2 teaspoon baking powder
1/2 teaspoon cinnamon
1/2 cup coconut oil or butter, softened
1/2 cup agave nectar or honey, at room temperature
1/4 teaspoon stevia glycerite (or increase brown sugar to 3/4 cup)
1/3 cup water

Preheat oven to 350 degrees. Spray a 9 by 13 inch glass baking dish with cooking spray.

In a small saucepan, combine the water, dates, salt, and stevia. Cook on medium-low heat for 15 minutes or until the mixture becomes a paste; stir often. Remove from the heat and set aside.

In a large bowl, stir together the oats, flour, wheat germ, brown sugar, salt, baking powder, and cinnamon.

In a separate bowl, whisk the coconut oil, agave, and stevia together. Add the wet ingredients to the dry ingredients, pour in the water and stir to combine. If the dough is dry and will not stick together when pinched between fingers, add a few more tablespoons of water or agave.

Press 2/3 of the the crust into the pan. Spread the date mixture on top, sprinkle with chocolate chips, then the top with the remaining crust. Bake for 30-40 minutes or until the top is lightly browned. Remove from the oven and let cool for 10 minutes before cutting.

Yield: 20 bars

CHOCOLATE TOPPED PEANUT BUTTER CEREAL SQUARES

2 teaspoons coconut oil or butter
1/2 cup organic corn syrup or brown rice syrup
1/4 cup non-hydrogenated peanut butter
2 cups marshmallows
1 teaspoon pure vanilla extract
3-1/2 cups crispy rice cereal
1 cup chocolate chips
1 tablespoon milk

Spray a 9 by 9 square baking dish with cooking spray.

In a large pot, melt the coconut oil on medium-low heat. Add the corn syrup, peanut butter, and marshmallows. Stir continuously until smooth. Remove from the heat stir in vanilla.

Add the cereal to the marshmallow mixture and stir to coat. Press into prepared dish and set aside.

Combine the chocolate chips and milk in a glass bowl and melt, either using a double boiler or microwave. If using a microwave, heat for 30 seconds at a time until melted, stirring in between heating. Spread chocolate on top of squares. Let cool thoroughly before cutting.

Yield: 9 bars

For <u>Chocolate Peanut Butter Squares:</u> Omit milk. Stir chocolate chips into the marshmallow mixture after adding cereal instead of topping squares with melted chocolate.

CEREAL SQUARES

This recipe is a lower in sugar and higher in fiber version of the original.

1 tablespoon coconut oil or butter
1/2 cup organic corn syrup or brown rice syrup
1/2 teaspoon stevia glycerite (or increase marshmallows to 2-1/2 cups)
2 cups marshmallows
1 teaspoon pure vanilla extract
2 cups crispy rice cereal
2 cups bran or high-fiber breakfast cereal

Grease a 9 by 9 inch baking dish and set aside.

In a large pot, melt coconut oil over medium-low heat. Add the corn syrup and stevia, stirring constantly. Add the marshmallows and stir until smooth. Remove from the heat and stir in the vanilla.

Measure the cereals into the marshmallow mixture and stir until completely coated. Immediately pour into the prepared pan and press down with a spatula. Let cool completely before cutting. Transfer to an airtight container.

Yield: 9 bars

For <u>Chocolate Chip Cereal Squares:</u> Mix in 1/2 cup chocolate chips after stirring in cereal.

For <u>Cranberry Cereal Squares:</u> Mix in 1/2 cup dried cranberries and 1/4 cup unsweetened shredded coconut after stirring in cereal.

PUMPKIN CHEESECAKE BARS

Crust:
1 cup whole wheat pastry flour
1/3 cup brown sugar
1/3 cup wheat germ or quick oats
5 tablespoons coconut oil or cold butter, cut into 1-inch pieces

Filling:
1 (8-ounce) container reduced-fat cream cheese
3/4 cup evaporated cane sugar OR 1/2 cup sugar and 1/4 teaspoon stevia glycerite
1-1/2 teaspoons ground cinnamon
1 teaspoon allspice
1/4 teaspoon ground ginger
1/2 cup pureed pumpkin
1 teaspoon pure vanilla extract
2 eggs or 1 egg and 2 egg whites

Preheat oven to 350 degrees. Grease an 8 by 8 inch baking dish.

Measure the flour, brown sugar, and wheat germ into a bowl. With a pastry cutter or a fork, incorporate the coconut oil into the dry ingredients, one piece at a time until it resembles coarse crumbs. Set 3/4 cup of mixture aside for topping.

Press the remaining mixture into the prepared pan. Bake for 15 minutes, remove from the oven, and set aside to cool while preparing the filling.

In a separate bowl, beat the cream cheese with a whisk until smooth. Add the sugar, cinnamon, allspice, ginger, and pumpkin and mix thoroughly. Stir in the vanilla and eggs. Pour the cream cheese mixture over the prepared crust and sprinkle with the reserved topping. Bake for 30 to 35 minutes. Remove from the oven and let cool completely before cutting. Serve with a dollop of Sweet Yogurt Cream (see below).

Yield: 9 servings

Sweet Yogurt Cream
1 cup Greek style yogurt or "yogurt cheese" (see glossary)
2 tablespoons honey or evaporated cane sugar or 1/8 teaspoon stevia glycerite
1/2 teaspoon pure vanilla extract

In a small bowl, mix the yogurt, honey, and vanilla together. Taste and adjust the sweetness to your liking. Refrigerate until ready to use.

For **Lemon or Almond Yogurt Cream:** Replace the vanilla extract with lemon or almond extract.

For **Cinnamon Yogurt Cream:** Stir 1/4 teaspoon cinnamon into the Sweet Yogurt Cream.

DESSERTS

Easy Chocolate Cake

Peach and Applesauce Cake

Chocolate Zucchini Cake

Super Moist Pumpkin Cake

Carrot Cake

Oatmeal Cake

Banana Cake

Fresh Fruit Cake

Pumpkin Pie with Gingersnap Crust

Rhuberry Crisp

When using milk in baked goods, choose from almond milk, coconut milk, organic cow's milk, or rice milk.

TIP: The recipes in this cookbook were created and tested in Denver. In Colorado, high altitude rules apply. If you don't live above 5000 feet, you may need to do one or more of the following for the baked goods to turn out well: increase the amount of baking powder or baking soda, decrease the oven temperature by 25 degrees, or decrease the amount of liquid by 2-3 tablespoons per cup of flour called for in the recipe. Baking and cooking times may need to be adjusted as well.

EASY CHOCOLATE CAKE

This dense, moist, one-bowl cake recipe is my favorite cake to make for birthdays. I like to use a mixture of Dutch process cocoa powder and natural cocoa powder for an intense chocolate flavor. I really enjoy the flavor of Dandy Blend Beverage (see glossary) to drink as a coffee replacement, and to add to baked goods. The vinegar may seem like an odd addition to a cake recipe but it is the secret ingredient.

1-1/2 cups all purpose flour
1/2 teaspoon baking soda
1 teaspoon baking powder
1/2 teaspoon salt
1 teaspoon instant powdered coffee replacement(optional)
3/4 cup unsweetened cocoa powder
1/2 cup plus 2 tablespoons brown sugar or evaporated cane sugar
3/4 cup unsweetened applesauce or Prune Puree (see index)
1/2 teaspoon stevia glycerite (or increase sugar by 1/2 cup)
2 eggs
1 teaspoon pure vanilla extract
1 cup milk
2 teaspoons white vinegar or balsamic vinegar

Preheat oven to 350 degrees. Grease a 9-inch round cake pan or place cupcake liners in 12-cups.

In a large bowl, combine the flour, baking soda, baking powder, salt, coffee powder, cocoa powder, and brown sugar and stir to mix. Measure the applesauce, stevia, eggs, vanilla, milk, and vinegar on top of the flour mixture. Stir gently to mix the wet and dry ingredients, then beat vigorously with a whisk until the mixture is smooth.

Pour into the prepared pan. Bake for 20 minutes for cupcakes or 25-30 minutes for cake or until a toothpick comes out clean. Remove from the oven and set on a cooling rack for 10 minutes before removing the cake from the pan.

Yield: 12 servings or 12 cupcakes

For a <u>Double Layer Chocolate Cake:</u> double the recipe and bake in two 9-inch round pans. Spread chocolate frosting or fruit juice sweetened raspberry jam on the bottom layer then top with the second cake. Frost with Chocolate Frosting (see index) or Marshmallow Fluff (see index)

TIP: To decrease the fat in muffin and cake recipes, replace 3/4 of the oil or butter with prune puree or applesauce. Prune puree works especially well in chocolate cakes, muffins, and cookies.

PEACH AND APPLESAUCE CAKE

Your guests will never guess that the secret ingredient in this recipe is white beans. This cake is moist, healthy, and delicious----perfect for kids birthday parties. This cake also tastes great with Chocolate or Vanilla Frosting (see index).

1/2 cup canned great northern or cannellini white beans, drained and rinsed
1/2 cup canned peaches, drained
1/2 cup unsweetened applesauce
2 tablespoons coconut oil or butter, softened
1/2 teaspoon stevia glycerite or increase brown sugar to 1 cup
1/2 cup agave nectar or honey
1/2 cup brown sugar
2 eggs
1-1/2 cups whole wheat pastry flour
1/4 teaspoon ground cloves
1/2 teaspoon cinnamon
1/2 teaspoon baking soda
1 teaspoon baking powder
1/2 teaspoon salt

Preheat oven to 350 degrees. Grease a 9-inch round cake pan or a 12-cup muffin pan (or use cupcake liners).

Pour the beans into a food processor or blender and puree for 10 seconds. Add the peaches, applesauce, coconut oil, stevia, and agave and blend for 30 seconds or until smooth. Transfer the mixture to a large bowl, stir in the brown sugar and eggs, and mix well. In a separate bowl, mix the flour, cloves, cinnamon, baking soda, baking powder, and salt. Pour the liquid mixture into the dry and stir just until moistened.

Pour the batter into the prepared pan. Bake for 18-20 minutes for cupcakes or 25 minutes for cake or until a toothpick comes out clean. Remove from the oven and transfer to a wire rack. Let cool for 10 minutes, loosen edges with a spatula and flip cake onto a serving plate to remove from the pan. Pour Vanilla Glaze(see below) on top and let it drip down the sides.

Yield: 12 cake servings, 12 cupcakes or 24 mini cupcakes

VANILLA GLAZE:

1 tablespoon butter or coconut oil
1/4 cup agave nectar or honey
1/2 cup powdered sugar
Dash salt
1 teaspoon pure vanilla extract

Combine the butter, agave nectar, powdered sugar, and salt in a small saucepan and set over low heat. Stir until the butter melts then remove from the heat and stir in the vanilla. Pour glaze over a slightly cooled cake.

For <u>Peach Applesauce Muffins:</u> Add 3/4 cup rolled or quick oats, 2 tablespoons wheat germ, and 1/2 cup raisins to the dry ingredients, and 1/4 cup milk the wet ingredients before combining. Stir just until moistened then pour into 12 greased muffin cups. Bake in a preheated 350 degree oven for 18-20 minutes or until a toothpick comes out clean. Omit the Vanilla Glaze

TIP: It is easy to make cupcakes out of a cake recipe. Simply place cupcake papers into 12 muffin tins and fill 3/4 full with cake batter. Reduce baking time to 18-20 minutes.

CHOCOLATE ZUCCHINI CAKE

This cake is lightly sweet and delicious even without frosting. To make this cake a sweeter treat, add 1/2 cup chocolate chips to the batter or frost with Chocolate Frosting (see index).

1 cup buttermilk or 1 cup milk plus 1 tablespoon lemon juice
1–3/4 cup whole wheat pastry flour
3/4 cup unsweetened cocoa powder
1 teaspoon baking soda
1/2 teaspoon baking powder
1 teaspoon salt
3/4 cup evaporated cane sugar or brown sugar
1 cup grated zucchini
1/4 teaspoon stevia glycerite or increase sugar to 1 cup
1/2 cup unsweetened applesauce
1 egg

Preheat oven to 350 degrees. Grease a 9-inch cake pan or line a 12-cup muffin pan with cupcake liners. If not using buttermilk, mix the milk and lemon juice in a large bowl and set aside for 10 minutes.

Mix the flour, cocoa powder, baking soda, baking powder, salt, and sugar in a large bowl. Wrap the grated zucchini in a piece of paper towel, squeeze to eliminate the excess liquid and place in a large bowl. Add the buttermilk, stevia, applesauce, and egg and stir well. Add the wet ingredients to the dry and stir just until moistened.

Pour into the prepared pan and bake for 20 minutes for cupcakes, or 25-30 minutes for cake or until a toothpick comes out clean.

Yield: 12 servings

TIP: To pack cupcakes in a lunch, cut the cupcakes in half, spread frosting on the bottom half, replace the other half on top and wrap in plastic wrap.

SUPER MOIST PUMPKIN CAKE

This "one bowl" cake using all purpose baking mix is really simple to make. Look for a baking mix that contains whole wheat flour to increase the nutrition. This cake is so deliciously moist that it doesn't even need icing. For a nice presentation, dish out a piece of cake onto a plate, top with sliced peaches or pears and add a dollop of Sweet Yogurt Cream (see index) or frozen non-dairy whipped topping.

2 cups canned or cooked and pureed fresh pumpkin
2 large eggs
1 cup milk
1/2 cup agave nectar or honey
1/4 cup brown sugar
1/4 tsp stevia glycerite or increase brown sugar to 1/2 cup
1-1/2 cups store-bought organic all purpose baking mix
2-1/2 teaspoons pumpkin pie spice
1/4 teaspoon salt

Preheat oven to 350 degrees. Grease a 9-inch round cake pan.

Mix the pumpkin, eggs, milk, agave, brown sugar, and stevia in a large bowl. Add the baking mix, pumpkin pie spice, and salt, then stir gently until smooth. Pour batter into the prepared pan and bake for 35 minutes or until a toothpick comes out clean.
Remove from the oven and set on a wire rack to cool. Serve this cake directly out of pan; it is too moist to remove as a whole.

Yield: 12 servings

CARROT CAKE

This moist carrot cake is especially delicious as a double layer cake with frosting between the layers. Make sure that the honey and applesauce are at room temperature if using coconut oil, to prevent hard oil lumps. The baby carrots can be replaced by increasing the applesauce to 1/2 cup.

3/4 cup buttermilk or 3/4 cup milk plus 2 teaspoons lemon juice
1–1/2 cups unbleached all purpose flour
2 cups whole wheat flour or whole wheat pastry flour
1/2 cup evaporated cane sugar
1/4 cup brown sugar
2 teaspoons cinnamon
1/2 teaspoon ground nutmeg
1/4 teaspoon ground cloves
1 teaspoon baking powder
2 teaspoons baking soda
1/4 teaspoon salt
1/4 cup grapeseed oil or melted coconut oil
1/2 cup honey or agave nectar, room temperature
1/4 cup applesauce, room temperature
2 eggs
1 cup crushed pineapple, drained
2 cups shredded carrots
1 (2–1/2–ounce) jar baby carrots or 1/4 cup pureed cooked carrots
1 cup raisins

Preheat oven to 350 degrees. Grease 2 round 8-inch cake pans. If not using buttermilk, mix the lemon juice and milk together in a small bowl and set aside.

In a large bowl mix the all purpose flour, whole wheat pastry flour, evaporated cane sugar, brown sugar, cinnamon, nutmeg, cloves, baking powder, baking soda, and salt; stir to combine.

In a separate bowl whisk the oil, honey, applesauce, and eggs, then stir vigorously to mix. Stir in the pineapple, carrots, pureed carrots, raisins, and buttermilk. Add the wet ingredients to the dry and stir gently.

Pour the batter into the prepared pans and bake for 30-40 minutes or until a toothpick comes out clean. Frost with Cream Cheese Frosting (see index).

Yield: 12 servings

TIP: *Place strips of wax paper under the cake when applying frosting to prevent it from dripping onto the cake platter. Remove the wax paper immediately after frosting.*

OATMEAL CAKE

This moist, healthy cake is delicious with the extra sweetness of the chopped dates(or apples, raisins or chocolate chips) and Vanilla Frosting or Vanilla Glaze (see index). It is a great snack cake even without the frosting and is simple to turn into muffins.

1 cup rolled oats
1 cup boiling water
1-1/2 cups whole wheat pastry flour
3/4 cup brown sugar
3/4 teaspoon salt
2 teaspoons baking powder
1 teaspoon cinnamon
1 cup chopped dates, diced apples, raisins, or chocolate chips
1/4 cup agave nectar or honey
1/2 teaspoon stevia glycerite (or increase brown sugar to 1 cup)
1 egg or 2 egg whites
1/2 cup unsweetened applesauce
1 teaspoon pure vanilla extract

Preheat oven to 350 degrees. Coat an 8-inch round cake pan with cooking spray. Combine the oats and water in a large bowl; stir and set aside. Measure the flour, brown sugar, salt, baking powder, cinnamon, and chopped dates into a separate bowl and mix. Add the agave, stevia, egg, applesauce, and vanilla to the oats and stir well. Add the wet ingredients to the dry and stir just until combined. Pour batter into the greased cake pan and bake for 25 minutes or until a toothpick comes out clean.

Yield: 9 servings

For Oatmeal Date Muffins: Divide the batter evenly between 12 greased muffin cups and reduce baking time to 18-20 minutes or until a toothpick comes out clean.

TIP: 1/2 cup chopped dates equals 3 large dates.

BANANA CAKE

My kids like to eat this deliciously moist cake even without the frosting. With a few additions, this cake recipe turns into tasty and nutritious muffins.

2 cups whole wheat pastry flour
1-1/4 teaspoons baking powder
1/2 teaspoon baking soda
1/2 teaspoon salt
1/4 cup plain low-fat yogurt
1/4 cup agave nectar or honey
1/2 cup brown sugar or evaporated cane sugar
1/2 cup unsweetened applesauce
1/4 teaspoon stevia glycerite or increase sugar to 3/4 cup
2 eggs
1-1/2 cups mashed bananas (about 3 medium)

Preheat oven to 350 degrees. Coat 2 (8-inch) round cake pans with cooking spray. Mix the flour, baking powder, baking soda, and salt in a large bowl.

In a separate bowl, whisk the yogurt, agave, and brown sugar together then stir in the stevia and eggs. Add the banana and whisk vigorously. Add the wet ingredients to the dry and stir just until moistened. Pour the batter into the prepared pans and bake for 20-25 minutes or until a toothpick comes out clean. Remove from the oven and let cool for 10 minutes before removing from the pan. Let cool completely before frosting.

To decorate the cake, spread a layer of Chocolate or Vanilla Frosting (see index) on one cake, top with sliced bananas, add the second cake and frost the top and sides.

Yield: 12 servings

For Banana Oatmeal Muffins: Add 3/4 cup rolled oats or quick oats, 2 tablespoons wheat germ or flaxseed meal, and 3/4 cup raisins or chocolate chips to the dry ingredients, and 1/4 cup milk to the wet ingredients, before mixing. Stir to combine and pour evenly into 12 greased muffin cups. Bake for 20 minutes or until a toothpick comes out clean.

TIP: *Freeze browning bananas with or without the peel. Thaw and drain the liquid before using in baked goods recipes.*

FRESH FRUIT CAKE

The inspiration for this cake came from a friend who makes a similar version for birthday parties. I spent months perfecting a moist and delicious, low-fat yellow cake recipe. I hope that you enjoy this cake as much as my family does. It is a perfect ending for a summer meal and looks impressive with the fresh fruit garnish. This basic yellow cake also tastes great with Chocolate Frosting(see index).

Yellow Cake:
1 cup unsweetened applesauce
2 eggs or 1 egg and 2 egg whites
2 teaspoons pure vanilla extract or 1 teaspoon vanilla extract and 1 teaspoon almond extract
1/2 teaspoon stevia glycerite (or increase evaporated cane sugar to 1 cup)
1-1/2 cups unbleached all purpose flour
1 cup whole wheat pastry flour
1/2 cup evaporated cane sugar
1/2 cup brown sugar
3/4 teaspoon salt
2 teaspoons baking powder
1 cup milk

1 double recipe Cream Cheese Frosting (see index)
3 cups mixed fresh fruit (strawberries, blueberries, raspberries, blackberries)

Preheat oven to 350 degrees. Spray 2 (8-inch) round cake pans with cooking spray.

In a large bowl, combine the applesauce, eggs, vanilla, and stevia and stir well. Measure the all purpose flour, whole wheat pastry flour, evaporated cane sugar, brown sugar, salt, baking powder, and milk on top of the dry ingredients and whisk vigorously until the mixture is smooth.

Pour into the prepared pans and bake for 25 minutes or until a toothpick comes out clean. Let cool on a wire rack for 10 minutes then remove from the pan.

While the cake is baking: slice the strawberries lengthwise in 1/4-inch slices, cut the raspberries or blackberries in half lengthwise and prepare the Cream Cheese Frosting (see index).

When the cake has cooled, spread a layer of frosting on the top of one cake and add a single layer of berries. Place the second cake on top and frost the top and sides of cake. Place the remaining berries on top and refrigerate until ready to serve.

Yield: 16 servings

For **Lemon Cake:** Reduce the vanilla extract to 1 teaspoon, add 1 teaspoon lemon extract and 1 teaspoon freshly grated lemon peel.

TIP: When icing a cake, let the cake cool completely then spread a thin layer of frosting over the entire cake to catch any loose crumbs. Let the first layer of icing dry for a few minutes then spread a thicker layer of frosting to cover the entire cake.

PUMPKIN PIE WITH GINGERSNAP CRUST

The rum definitely adds a distinct flavor. If you don't like rum, replace it with 2 teaspoons pure vanilla extract. Serve this pie with non-dairy frozen whipped topping or vanilla ice cream. This pie can be made the day before and refrigerated until ready to serve.

Crust:
1 cup graham cracker crumbs (8–9 graham cracker sheets)
1/2 cup gingersnap crumbs (or increase graham crumbs to 1–1/2 cups)
1 tablespoon evaporated cane sugar
Dash salt
2 tablespoons coconut oil or butter
1 tablespoon milk

Filling:
2 cups pumpkin (fresh or canned)
1/2 cup light coconut milk or soymilk
1/2 cup maple syrup or honey
1/4 teaspoon stevia glycerite or 1/4 cup evaporated cane sugar
2 eggs
2 teaspoons pumpkin pie spice
1/2 teaspoon cinnamon
1/8 teaspoon salt
1 tablespoon light rum (optional)
1 tablespoon arrowroot or cornstarch

Preheat oven to 350 degrees. Coat a 9-inch pie plate with cooking spray.

To make crumbs: break the graham crackers and gingersnaps into pieces then whip in a blender on high speed to pulverize, or place sheets in a plastic bag and crush with a rolling pin.

Place graham cracker crumbs, gingersnap crumbs, salt, and sugar into a bowl and stir to mix. Using a pastry cutter or a fork, cut in the coconut oil then stir in the milk. Press into the prepared pie plate and bake for 6-8 minutes. Remove from the oven and set aside.

Measure the pumpkin, milk, maple syrup, stevia, eggs, pumpkin pie spice, cinnamon, salt, rum, and arrowroot into a blender or food processor and mix for 10-15 seconds until smooth.

Pour the filling into the cooled pie crust and bake for 60-75 minutes until the center is set. If the crust is browning too quickly, cover the edges with aluminum foil. Remove from the oven and let cool before serving.

Yield: 8 servings

RHUBERRY CRISP

Filling:
2 cups rhubarb (fresh or frozen)
1/4 cup evaporated cane sugar
1/4 teaspoon liquid stevia glycerite or increase sugar to 1/2 cup
1/4 cup agave nectar or honey
3-4 cups fresh or frozen blueberries or berry of your choice
1/8 teaspoon ground cinnamon
1 tablespoon arrowroot powder or cornstarch

Crisp Topping:
3/4 cup rolled oats
1 tablespoon wheat germ
1/4 cup whole wheat pastry flour
1/4 teaspoon salt
1/4 cup brown sugar
2 tablespoons coconut oil
2 tablespoons agave nectar or honey

Preheat oven to 350 degrees. Coat a 9 by 9 inch glass baking dish with cooking spray.

In a medium saucepan mix the rhubarb, sugar, stevia, and agave nectar, and set on medium-low heat. Cook and stir for 5 minutes or until the rhubarb is fork-tender.

While the rhubarb is cooking, measure the oats, wheat germ, flour, salt, and brown sugar into a medium bowl. With a fork or pastry cutter, mix in the coconut oil thoroughly then stir in the agave nectar.

Combine the berries and cinnamon in a large bowl. Stir in the arrowroot then add the rhubarb mixture; stir to combine. Pour fruit mixture into the prepared dish. Top with oatmeal mixture and bake for 45 minutes or until topping is crisp and browned.

Yield: 9 servings

For Apple Crisp: In a medium saucepan combine 4-5 cups unpeeled apples (cut into 1-inch pieces), 1 teaspoon cinnamon, 1/2 teaspoon stevia glycerite, 1/4 cup brown sugar, 1/4 cup agave nectar, and 1/4 cup raisins. Cook for 5 minutes, stirring often, then pour into a greased baking dish. Top with above "crisp topping" and bake for 45 minutes or until the top is nicely browned.

For Berry Crisp: Increase berries to 5-6 cups (mixture of your choice) and omit the rhubarb. Measure the above filling ingredients into a large bowl (decrease sugar by 2 tablespoons). Pour into a greased baking dish and top with "crisp topping". Bake for 45 minutes or until the top is brown and crisp.

FROSTINGS AND GLAZES

CHAPTER THIRTEEN

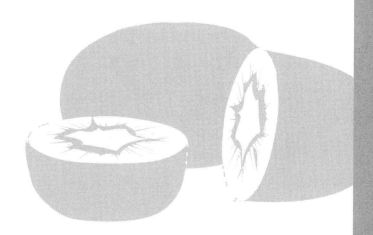

TIP: To save time on cake decorating, prepare the frosting up to three days before, cover with plastic wrap and refrigerate. Let sit at room temperature to soften, and stir well before spreading on a cooled cake.

CHOCOLATE FROSTING

The sour cream in this frosting gives it a silky smooth appearance and texture. Keep this frosting refrigerated because of the sour cream. This recipe is enough to frost 1 (9-inch) cake.

1/4 cup butter, softened
1/2 teaspoon stevia glycerite or increase powdered sugar to 3-1/2 cups
1/4 cup low-fat sour cream
1-1/4 cups unsweetened cocoa powder
1 teaspoon pure vanilla extract
3 cups powdered sugar

Cream the butter and with an electric mixer, or a whisk, in a large bowl. Add the stevia and sour cream and blend on low speed. Add the cocoa powder and vanilla and blend on medium speed until creamy. Mix in the powdered sugar 1/2 cup at a time, stirring well after each addition. Adjust the consistency to your liking by adding one teaspoon of milk or agave at a time to thin, or powdered sugar to thicken.

TIP: For a nice presentation. shave chocolate curls on top of a frosted cake using a carrot peeler and a dark chocolate bar.

CHOCOLATE HONEY GLAZE

This ooey-gooey sweet glaze is delicious on a chocolate, yellow, or carrot cake. This recipe will cover 1 (9-inch) cake.

1/2 cup agave nectar or honey
1/2 cup unsweetened cocoa powder
2 tablespoons semi-sweet or dark chocolate chips
1/2 teaspoon pure vanilla extract

Combine the agave nectar and cocoa powder in a small saucepan, set on low heat, and whisk to mix. Add the chocolate chips and stir until melted and the mixture is smooth. Remove from the heat, stir in the vanilla and pour over a cooled cake.

WHITE FLUFF FROSTING

This light, fluffy icing tastes great over a chocolate cake. This recipe is enough to frost 1 (9-inch) cake.

1 egg white
1/4 cup honey or agave nectar
1/8 teaspoon salt
1/2 teaspoon pure vanilla or almond extract
1/4 cup marshmallows

Fill a medium soup pot one third full of water and bring to a boil. Place a stainless steel bowl on top of the pot and add the egg white, honey, salt, and vanilla. Using an electric mixer, beat for 3-4 minutes until the mixture thickens and forms soft peaks. Add the marshmallows and beat continuously until melted (using the mixer or a whisk). Remove the bowl and whisk vigorously for a few more minutes while the mixture starts to cool. Set aside to cool completely then spread frosting over a cooled yellow or chocolate cake.

COCOA DATE FROSTING

No one will guess that this frosting is low in sugar and is made with dates. This recipe will cover 1 (8-inch) cake. This thick, rich frosting is especially delicious between the layers of a double layer cake.

8-10 dates, stems and pits removed
1/2 cup unsweetened apple juice
1/4 cup milk
2 tablespoons coconut oil or butter
3/. cup unsweetened cocoa powder
3/4 teaspoon stevia glycerite
1/2 teaspoon pure vanilla extract
3 tablespoons agave nectar or honey
Dash salt

Place the dates and apple juice in a small saucepan and simmer for 5 minutes. Transfer to a blender and add the milk and coconut oil. Puree for 15-30 seconds until the mixture is smooth.

Transfer the date mixture to a bowl and stir in the cocoa powder, stevia, vanilla, agave nectar and salt. Mix vigorously until creamy. Thin the frosting by adding agave, if necessary. Spread over a cooled chocolate cake.

LEMON CREAM CHEESE FROSTING

This frosting can be made ahead of time and refrigerated for up to a week, or frozen for a few months. Thaw and stir before using. This frosting will cover 1 (9-inch) double layer cake.

3 tablespoons softened butter
1 (8-ounce) package reduced-fat cream cheese, softened
1 tablespoon low-fat sour cream
1 teaspoon lemon extract
1/2 teaspoon freshly grated lemon peel
2 cups powdered sugar

In a bowl, beat the butter and cream cheese until smooth then stir in the sour cream and lemon extract. Add the powdered sugar, 1/2 cup at a time, then mix in the lemon peel. Adjust the consistency by adding powdered sugar to thicken or a teaspoon of milk to thin.

For <u>Vanilla Cream Cheese Frosting</u>: Replace the lemon extract with pure vanilla extract and omit the lemon peel.

Yield: about 3 cups

TIP: *To make your own powdered sugar, blend evaporated cane sugar in a blender until superfine.*

POWDERED MILK FROSTING

The sweetness of the stevia allows for the amount of powdered sugar to be reduced and the dry milk powder helps to thicken the frosting. This recipe is enough to cover 1 (9-inch) cake.

2 tablespoons softened butter
1 (8-ounce) package softened reduced-fat cream cheese
1/2 teaspoon stevia glycerite or increase powdered sugar to 1-1/2 cups
2 teaspoons pure vanilla, lemon or almond extract
3/4 cup powdered milk
1 cup powdered sugar
Dash salt

Beat the butter, cream cheese, and stevia in a bowl until smooth and fluffy. Add the vanilla, milk powder, and powdered sugar, and stir well. Adjust the consistency by adding more powdered sugar or honey. Spread over a cooled cake.

CHOCOLATE CREAM CHEESE FROSTING

This thick, silky smooth frosting is perfect for a Yellow Cake, Chocolate Cake, or Banana Cake. For an even richer flavor, use a combination of Dutch process cocoa powder and natural cocoa powder. If not using stevia, increase the powdered sugar and milk to your desired consistency. This recipe is enough to frost 1 (9-inch) cake.

4-ounces reduced-fat cream cheese, softened
1/4 cup low-fat sour cream
2 tablespoons agave nectar
1/2 teaspoon pure vanilla extract
1/4 cup unsweetened cocoa powder
Dash salt
1/2 cup powdered sugar
1 teaspoon milk
1/4 teaspoon stevia glycerite or increase powdered sugar to 3/4 cup

In a large bowl, beat the cream cheese until smooth. Whisk in the sour cream, agave, and vanilla then stir in the cocoa powder, salt, powdered sugar, milk, and stevia. Whisk vigorously until very smooth and creamy.

Yield: 1-1/2 cups

TIP: To toast coconut, preheat oven to 350 degrees. Spread unsweetened shredded coconut onto an ungreased cookie sheet. Bake for 5-7 minutes or until the coconut is golden. It will burn quickly so stir every few minutes while toasting, and check often.

VANILLA FROSTING

This creamy frosting recipe is enough to cover 1 (9-inch) cake.

1/4 cup butter, softened
1 tablespoon agave nectar or honey
1/2 teaspoon stevia glycerite or increase powdered sugar to 3 cups
1 teaspoon pure vanilla extract
2 tablespoons low-fat sour cream
2-1/2 cups powdered sugar
Dash salt

In a medium bowl, mix the butter, honey, and stevia together using an electric mixer or a whisk. Mix in the vanilla and sour cream until the mixture is creamy, then add the powdered sugar. Stir until smooth. If using all powdered sugar instead of stevia, increase sour cream to 3 tablespoons. Spread over a cooled cake.

For <u>Coconut Frosting:</u> Stir in 3/4 cup unsweetened shredded coconut. For an intense coconut flavor, replace the vanilla extract with coconut extract, or replace 2 tablespoons of the butter with coconut oil.

MISCELLANEOUS

CHAPTER FOURTEEN

Brown Sugar Spice Rub
Nic's Mix
Apricot Dijon Dipping Sauce
Teriyaki Sauce
Honey Barbeque Sauce
Pure Vanilla Extract
Prune Puree
Crispy Coating
Garlic Parsley Croutons
Tzatziki Sauce
Chunky Applesauce
Basil Sauce
Mango Peach Salsa
Fresh Garden Salsa
Spiced Cranberry Sauce
Cranberry Chutney
Pasta Sauce
Balsamic Glaze
Honey Mustard Sauce
Bourbon Sauce
Cheese Spread
Nacho Cheese Dip
Apple Cider Vinegar Drink
Lemonade Soda

BROWN SUGAR SPICE RUB

This rub caramelizes beautifully and tastes great on pork, chicken, and salmon. Mix up extra rub, excluding the oil, and store it in an airtight container. This mixture is enough to season 1 pound of meat.

2 tablespoons brown sugar
2 teaspoons chili powder
1–1/2 teaspoons salt
1/2 teaspoon garlic powder
1/2 teaspoon ground cumin
1/4 teaspoon ground ginger
1/4 teaspoon ground cinnamon
1/4 teaspoon ground black pepper
1/4 teaspoon dry mustard
1/2 teaspoon smoked paprika or sweet paprika
4 teaspoons extra virgin olive oil

Combine the brown sugar, chili powder, salt, garlic powder, cumin, ginger, cinnamon, pepper, dry mustard, and paprika in a medium bowl. Stir well to mix then transfer to an airtight container. To use the rub: stir in the olive oil, mixing with a spoon to incorporate oil completely. Rub mixture onto all sides of the meat and grill until cooked.

NIC'S MIX

This is my own version of seasoning salt. I use it to season homemade chips, dips, cooked veggies, and season meat or chicken before or during cooking.

2 tablespoons garlic salt
1 tablespoon paprika
1 tablespoon chili powder
2 teaspoons onion salt
1 teaspoon dried oregano
1 teaspoon dried basil
1 teaspoon thyme
1/2 teaspoon allspice
2 teaspoons salt
1/4 teaspoon black pepper
1/2 teaspoon dry mustard
1/4 teaspoon evaporated cane sugar
1 teaspoon celery seed

Mix all the ingredients together in a bowl and stir well. Transfer to a spice jar or airtight container.

Yield: about 1/3 cup

APRICOT DIJON DIPPING SAUCE

Serve this sauce with Coconut Chicken Fingers(see index) or Coconut Shrimp

1/2 cup fruit juice sweetened apricot jam
1/4 cup honey or agave nectar
3 tablespoons Dijon-styl. mustard
Dash hot sauce

Mix the jam, honey, mustard, and hot sauce together in a small bowl and serve as a dipping sauce.

Yield: about 1 cup

TERIYAKI SAUCE

This thick, sweet sauce can be basted onto chicken or pork while cooking or used as a stir-fry sauce. Store in a sealed container in the refrigerator for up to 2 weeks.

1/3 cup soy sauce or tamari
1/2 cup pineapple juice or orange juice
1/4 cup ketchup
2 tablespoons rice vinegar
1/4 cup brown sugar
3 tablespoons honey or agave nectar
1/2 teaspoon minced ginger
1/2 teaspoon minced garlic
1/4 teaspoon crushed red pepper flakes (add more for spicy)
2 teaspoons sesame seeds

Combine the soy sauce, pineapple juice, ketchup, rice vinegar, brown sugar, honey, ginger, garlic, and red pepper flakes in a large saucepan. Simmer over medium-low heat for 5-10 minutes until reduced and slightly thickened. Stir in the sesame seeds and transfer to a glass container. Refrigerate until ready to use.

Yield: about 3/4 cup

PURE VANILLA EXTRACT

Making your own vanilla is easy and economical. I haven't bought vanilla extract in years!

Using a sharp knife, split a vanilla bean lengthwise. Leave the seeds in the bean. Place the split bean in a dark colored glass jar with a lid or cork. The bean can be cut into 1-inch pieces if necessary. Fill the jar with vodka or brandy. Use 1 vanilla bean per 1/2 cup of alcohol. Let the jar sit in a dark place for 2-4 weeks before using, shake daily. The extract should have an intense vanilla smell when it is ready. If there are loose vanilla seeds, strain the liquid, then return to the jar. Store in a dark, cool place and use as you would store-bought vanilla.

PRUNE PUREE

This mixture can be used to replace 3/4 of the fat (oil or butter) in baking. It is especially good in chocolate cookies and cakes. Lecithin helps to give baked goods moisture and texture but it is not necessary.

1 cup prunes, or a mixture of prunes and dates, pits removed
1 cup warm water
1 tablespoon liquid lecithin, lecithin granules, or coconut oil (optional)

Combine the prunes and boiling water in a glass bowl and set aside for 10-15 minutes. Transfer the prunes and water to a blender or food processor. Add the lecithin and puree until smooth. Pour into an airtight container and store in the fridge for up to two weeks, or freeze for up to 3 months.

CRISPY COATING

This coating can be used to make crispy potatoes or cauliflower, or as a breading for chicken, shrimp or fish. Prepare extra and keep it in your pantry or freezer to decrease meal prep time.

1/4 cup finely ground cornmeal or crushed cornflake cereal
3 tablespoons unbleached all purpose flour
3 tablespoons toasted wheat germ or flaxseed meal
1 cup dry whole wheat or Panko bread crumbs
2 teaspoons evaporated cane sugar
1-1/2 teaspoons salt
1/2 teaspoon garlic salt
1 teaspoon dried basil
1 teaspoon dried oregano
1 teaspoon dried parsley
1/2 teaspoon onion powder
3 tablespoons grated Parmesan cheese

Measure all the ingredients into a bowl and stir well to mix. Store in an airtight container in the freezer until ready to use.

To make <u>Crispy Coated Vegetables:</u> coat vegetables lightly with extra virgin olive oil and toss with the coating. Coat with cooking spray and bake in a preheated 425 degree oven until fork-tender and brown and crispy.

To make <u>Crispy Coated Chicken or Fish:</u> brush with extra virgin olive oil and cover both sides with coating. Spray with cooking spray and bake in a preheated 425 degree oven until cooked through, golden brown, and crispy.

Yield: about 1-1/2 cups

TIP: Coating the vegetables or meats with cooking spray before baking or roasting helps them to become brown and crispy when cooking.

GARLIC PARSLEY CROUTONS

Homemade croutons are simple to make and add a nice crunch to a green salad or a bowl of hearty soup. Rye bread or sourdough bread also work well.

1 teaspoon salt
1/4 teaspoon evaporated cane sugar
1 teaspoon garlic powder
1/2 teaspoon onion salt
1-1/2 teaspoons dried parsley
8 slices of sprouted grain or whole wheat bread
2 tablespoons extra virgin olive oil

Preheat oven to 325 degrees.

Combine the salt, sugar, garlic powder, onion salt, and dried parsley in a small bowl.

Brush olive oil on one side of each slice of bread and cut into bite-size pieces. Place the bread in a large bowl and toss with the seasoning mixture. Pour the bread pieces onto a baking sheet and spread out into a single layer. Spray with cooking spray and bake for 30-35 minutes, flipping pieces at 10 and 20 minutes. Remove the pan from the oven, let cool completely, then transfer to an airtight container for up to 2 weeks.

Yield: 10 cups

TZATZIKI SAUCE

This cool cucumber sauce is great with Baked Falafel(see index) and grilled chicken. Greek style yogurt is very thick so it can be used straight out of the container instead of straining it. For a quick version, use plain low-fat yogurt. The sauce will be thinner but still delicious.

2 cups yogurt cheese(see glossary) or Greek style yogurt
1/2 large English cucumber, grated
1/2 teaspoon salt
2 teaspoons minced garlic
2 tablespoons low–fat sour cream
1 teaspoon white vinegar
1 teaspoon lemon juice
1/2 teaspoon salt
Dash freshly ground black pepper
1 teaspoon extra virgin olive oil
1 teaspoon dried parsley or 1 tablespoon chopped fresh parsley

Grate the unpeeled cucumber into a colander and sprinkle with salt; stir. Set the colander over a bowl and refrigerate for 1-2 hours then discard the liquid from bottom of the bowl. In a separate bowl, mix the minced garlic, sour cream, vinegar, lemon juice, salt, pepper, olive oil, and parsley. Add the yogurt and cucumber and stir well. Refrigerate for 1 hour before serving.

Yield: about 3 cups

TIP: *Mixing the cucumber with salt will draw out the liquid and prevent the sauce from becoming watery.*

CHUNKY APPLESAUCE

This sauce is delicious with grilled pork or chicken.

3 apples, unpeeled and chopped into bite-size pieces
2 tablespoons finely diced yellow onion
1/4 cup water
1/2 cup maple syrup
2 tablespoons evaporated cane sugar or 1/8 teaspoon liquid stevia glycerite
1 teaspoon ground cinnamon
1/4 teaspoon ground cloves
1/4 teaspoon lemon juice
1/2 teaspoon salt
Dash of black pepper
1/4 cup raisins (optional)

Measure the apples, onion, water, maple syrup, sugar, cinnamon, cloves, lemon juice, salt, pepper, and raisins into a medium saucepan. Simmer on medium-low heat for 20 minutes or until the apples are really tender; stir often. Remove from the heat and serve warm, or refrigerate to serve cold.

BASIL SAUCE

This is a great dipping sauce for steamed or Grilled Artichokes or roasted asparagus or drizzled over chicken.

1/2 cup low-fat mayonnaise
1/2 cup plain low-fat yogurt or sour cream
1/4 cup chopped fresh basil or 1 tablespoon dried basil
1 tablespoon lemon juice
1 clove garlic, minced
1 teaspoon extra virgin olive oil
Salt and pepper to taste

Mix the mayonnaise, yogurt, basil, lemon juice, garlic, and olive oil in a small bowl. Add salt and pepper to your liking. Serve cold or at room temperature.

Yield: about 1 cup

MANGO PEACH SALSA

Serve this fresh salsa over grilled chicken or with tortilla chips. Gently squeezing the tomatoes reduces the excess liquid which makes the salsa thick instead of watery.

2 large (about 3 cups) tomatoes
1/2 cup diced mango
1/2 cup diced peaches
1/4 cup diced red onion
1/2 red bell pepper, diced
1-2 teaspoons chopped jalapeno pepper
2 teaspoons lime juice
1 tablespoon evaporated cane sugar
2 tablespoons chopped fresh cilantro
Salt to taste
Dash hot sauce

Cut the tops off of the tomatoes and gently squeeze upside down over a bowl or a sink to remove excess liquid. Dice the tomatoes and set aside. In a large bowl, mix the mango, peaches, onion, red bell pepper, jalapeno, and tomatoes. Stir in the lime juice, sugar, cilantro, salt, and hot sauce. Taste and adjust to your liking. Refrigerate to cool.

Yield: about 5 cups

FRESH GARDEN SALSA

Salsa from a jar doesn't even compare to fresh. This salsa is easy and quick to make.

6 medium tomatoes (4-5 cups)
1/2 cup diced red onion
1/4 cup diced red bell pepper
1 tomatillo, husked and diced (optional)
2 tablespoons fresh lime juice
2 tablespoons fresh orange juice
2 tablespoons chopped jalapeno pepper
1 teaspoon evaporated cane sugar
2 tablespoons chopped fresh cilantro
Salt to taste

Cut the tops off of the tomatoes, hold cut side down over the sink or a bowl, and gently squeeze to reduce excess liquid. Dice the tomatoes and place in a large bowl. Add the onion, red pepper, tomatillo, lime juice, orange juice, jalapeno, sugar, and cilantro, then stir. Add salt to taste and refrigerate to cool.

Yield: 5-6 cups

TIP: When chopping herbs with soft stems (basil, cilantro, mint), you can use the stems and leaves. When using herbs with tough or woody stems(rosemary). us. the leaves only.

SPICED CRANBERRY SAUCE

If you prefer plain Cranberry Sauce, eliminate the cinnamon, cloves, and ginger.

2 cups (8-ounces) fresh cranberries
1 cup water
1/2 cup maple syrup or agave nectar
1/4 cup orange juice
2 tablespoons evaporated cane sugar or 1/8 teaspoon liquid stevia glycerite
1/2 teaspoon ground cinnamon
1/4 teaspoon ground cloves
1/8 teaspoon ground ginger
Dash salt

In a medium saucepan, bring the cranberries and water to a boil. Reduce heat to medium-low and simmer until the berries start to pop. Stir in the agave, orange juice, sugar, cinnamon, cloves, and ginger, then cook for 10 more minutes or until thickened slightly. Taste and adjust sweetness to your liking then remove from the heat. Serve warm or cold.

Yield: 2 cups

CRANBERRY CHUTNEY

Serve this chutney as a Thanksgiving condiment, or with whipped cream cheese and whole grain crackers for an easy appetizer.

1/4 cup dried apricots, diced
2 tablespoons minced yellow onion
1/2 cup maple syrup
1/2 cup brown sugar or 1/2 teaspoon stevia glycerite
1/4 cup raisins
1/2 cup ruby port or apple juice
1/2 cup water
3 cups (12-ounces) fresh cranberries
1 medium apple, peeled and diced (about 3/4 cup)
1 teaspoon freshly grated lemon peel
2 tablespoons diced crystallized ginger or 1/2 teaspoon ground ginger
1/2 teaspoon cinnamon
1/8 teaspoon ground cloves
1/4 teaspoon dry mustard
1/8 teaspoon salt
Dash hot sauce

In a saucepan, combine the apricots, onion, maple syrup, sugar, raisins, ruby port, and water. Bring to a boil then reduce heat; let simmer for 5 minutes, stirring occasionally. Stir in the cranberries, apple, lemon peel, ginger, cinnamon, cloves, mustard, salt, and hot sauce. Simmer on medium-low heat for 10-15 minutes until the berries pop and the chutney thickens, stirring occasionally. Add more sweetener to taste then remove from the heat. Serve warm, or refrigerate to serve cold.

Yield: 3-1/2 cups

PASTA SAUCE

This recipe makes a big batch of sauce. Pour it over your favorite pasta and vegetables and freeze the rest!

1 tablespoon extra virgin olive oil
1 medium yellow onion, diced (about 1 cup)
3 cloves garlic, minced (3 teaspoons)
6 button mushrooms, quartered
1/2 green pepper, diced
1/2 red bell pepper, diced
3 (15-ounce) cans diced tomatoes or 6 cups fresh tomatoes, diced
1 (15-ounce) can tomato sauce or tomato puree
6-ounces tomato paste
1 tablespoon dried basil
1 tablespoon dried oregano
1 teaspoon dried marjoram
1/4 cup red wine
2 teaspoons salt
1/4 teaspoon freshly ground black pepper
2 tablespoons evaporated cane sugar or 1/4 teaspoon liquid stevia glycerite
2 tablespoons grated Parmesan cheese

In a large saucepan, heat the oil on medium heat. Cook and stir the onion and garlic for a few minutes then add the mushrooms, green pepper, and red pepper. Cook and stir for 5 minutes then add the tomatoes, tomato sauce, tomato paste, basil, oregano, marjoram, red wine, salt, pepper, and sugar. Simmer on medium-low heat for 1 hour until thickened, stirring occasionally. Stir in the cheese and remove from the heat. Store leftover sauce in a glass dish in the refrigerator or freeze in a freezer-safe container.

Yield: about 10 cups

TIP: Use glass dishes and containers instead of plastic to microwave food and to store liquid leftovers to avoid the leaching of toxic chemicals into your food.

BALSAMIC GLAZE

This sweet and tangy reduction is delicious drizzled on chicken, lamb, salmon, or roasted vegetables.

1-1/2 cups balsamic vinegar
3 tablespoons brown sugar or agave nectar
3 whole garlic cloves, peeled

In a small saucepan, mix the vinegar, brown sugar, and garlic. Bring to a boil then reduce heat to medium-low. Simmer for about 15 minutes or until the sauce is reduced by half (start timing after the mixture comes to a boil). Remove the garlic cloves and set aside. Drizzle glaze over the entrée, or on the outside inch of each plate for an impressive presentation.

Yield: 3/4 cup

For <u>Rosemary Balsamic Glaze:</u> Add 3 whole sprigs of rosemary to sauce. Remove after the glaze has thickened.

TIP: If you like garlic, save the cloves after removing from the glaze. They are delicious and sweet. Eat the whole clove or mash them and spread on fresh, whole grain crusty bread.

HONEY MUSTARD SAUCE

Serve this sauce with Crispy Chicken Fingers(see index).

2 tablespoons low-fat mayonnaise, sour cream, or yogurt
1/4 cup prepared mustard
1/4 cup honey

Whisk the mayonnaise and mustard in a small bowl, then stir in the honey. Refrigerate for up to one week.

Yield: 1/2 cup

BOURBON SAUCE

This sauce is simple to make is wonderful drizzled on grilled pork or chicken.

1/2 cup maple syrup
1/3 cup bourbon or apple juice
3 tablespoons Dijon mustard
2 tablespoons ketchup

In a small saucepan mix the maple syrup, bourbon, mustard and ketchup. Bring to a boil, reduce the heat, and simmer for 10 minutes or until the sauce has thickened. Remove from the heat and transfer to a bowl and serve. Refrigerate the remaining sauce in an airtight container for up to a week.

Yield: about 3/4 cup

CHEESE SPREAD

This yummy cheese spread can be used on toast or crackers or used as a sauce. To make Cheese Sauce, combine some of the spread with a few tablespoons of milk in a saucepan and heat on medium-low heat until pourable. Mix the sauce with whole wheat noodles, or pour over steamed or roasted vegetables.

2 eggs or 1 egg and 2 egg whites
4 cups (about 1 pound) sharp cheddar cheese (shredded or cut into small pieces)
1 (12-ounce) can evaporated skim milk (1-1/2 cups)
1-1/2 teaspoons salt
2 teaspoons dry mustard or prepared yellow mustard

Break the eggs into a medium bowl, beat lightly, and set aside.

Place the cheese into a large saucepan or double boiler and set over medium-low heat. Stir and cook until the cheese has melted. Add the milk, 1/4 cup at a time, whisking after each addition, then whisk in the salt and mustard.

While stirring, pour 1/2 cup cheese mixture into the eggs. Pour the eggs back into the saucepan, increase to medium-high, and stir continuously for 5 minutes or until the mixture has thickened slightly; do not boil. Remove from the heat, let cool slightly, then transfer to a glass bowl and cover with a lid. The mixture will firm up as it cools. This will keep for several weeks in the fridge.

TIP: If the mixture boils, it will curdle. Pour mixture into a blender and blend on high for a few seconds until smooth.

NACHO CHEESE DIP

1 cup Cheese Spread (see index)
1 cup salsa

Melt the cheese spread in a saucepan then mix in the salsa. Add a few tablespoons of milk to thin, if desired. Serve with whole grain crackers or tortilla chips.

APPLE CIDER VINEGAR DRINK

When you are feeling under the weather, sip this zesty, healthful drink. It will help to cure what ails you. Add as much apple cider vinegar as you can tolerate.

1 cup water
2 teaspoons lemon juice
1 tablespoon raw apple cider vinegar
1 (2-inch) piece fresh ginger, peele.
Dash cayenne pepper
Raw honey or stevia glycerite to taste

Mix the water, lemon juice, vinegar, ginger and cayenne in a small saucepan and simmer on low heat for a few minutes. Pour into a mug, add sweetener, and sip often.

Yield: 1 serving

LEMONADE SODA

This sweet, sugarless drink is a good way to increase your water intake without drinking empty calories.

16-ounces water or sparkling water
2 tablespoons lemon juice
1/4 teaspoon stevia glycerite

Mix water, lemon juice, and stevia together. Adjust lemon juice and stevia to your desired sweetness.

For Minty Lemon Soda: Add fresh mint to lemonade. For a slushy drink, puree in a blender with ice.

GLOSSARY OF TERMS

<u>Agave Nectar</u> - sweetener similar in taste to honey. It has a thinner consistency and lower glycemic index. Use cup for cup instead of honey. If using to replace sugar, decrease liquid by 1/4 cup. Refer to the "Sweeteners" section of the introduction for more information.
Brand Recommendation: Madhava

<u>All Purpose Baking Mix</u> - a pre-mixed combination of ingredients to which liquid is added to make muffins, cakes and biscuits. It contains properly measured ingredients to result in predictable, good results. An all purpose baking mix can be handy to have in your pantry if you are short on time or would prefer to have the ingredients already measured out for you. Look for organic baking mixes that contain whole wheat flour to increase fiber and nutrients. Avoid hydrogenated or chemical ingredients.
Brand Recommendation: Arrowhead Mills

<u>Almond Milk</u> - creamy, non-dairy beverage made from almonds. It is a delicious alternative to cow and soy milk. It is available in original, unsweetened, vanilla and chocolate on the shelf in asceptic containers. I buy it by the case and use it daily to drink and to replace cow's milk in recipes. It is sold in traditional grocery stores and health food stores.
Brand Recommendations: Almond Breeze and Pacific Natural Foods

<u>Arrowroot</u> - thickener that is easily digestible and high in minerals. It is derived from the tuber root of a tropical American plant. Use 1-1/2 tablespoons for every 1 cup of liquid. Use instead of cornstarch to thicken sauces, puddings, and pie fillings. 1 tablespoon of cornstarch equals 1 tablespoon arrowroot. Needs to be cooked for several minutes on low heat to thicken.

<u>Barley Malt</u> - a mild sweetener made from sprouted barley. It is similar to molasses in consistency and color. Add a small amount to breads to for a chewy, bagel-like texture.

<u>Bread Flour</u> - high-gluten flour that provides chewiness to breads. Mix bread flour with whole wheat flour to give breads "lift.. Unbleached all-purpose flour can be used in place of bread flour.

<u>Brown rice</u> - Whole, unpolished rice that still has the bran and germ.

<u>Brown Rice Syrup</u> - mild sweet golden syrup. It is made by reducing brown rice in filtered water. It can replace sugar, honey, corn syrup, maple syrup, or molasses. Use 1-1/4 cup rice syrup for one cup of sugar and reduce liquid by 1/4 cup. **Brand Recommendation:** Lundberg

Brown sugar(organic) - freshly cut organic sugarcane is milled, crushed, purified, and crystallized with no artificial preservatives or additives. It retains more nutrients than conventional brown sugar which is just refined sugar covered in molasses.
Brand Recommendation. Hain Pure Foods

Buttermilk - low-fat milk with a creamy texture. It has a less tangy taste than yogurt. It can be added to soups, sauces, or baked goods without needing to add much extra sugar. If you don't have buttermilk mix 1 tablespoon lemon juice with 1 cup milk and set aside for 10 minutes to thicken. It is available in liquid form in the refrigerated section, and on the shelf in powdered form.

Cannellini beans - a white kidney bean with a mild flavor. They can be used interchangeably with great northern beans or navy beans in most recipes.

Chickpeas(garbanzo beans/ceci beans) - are a member of the legume family. They have a firm texture and mild nutty taste. Chickpeas are high in fiber, folate, and magnesium and provide small amounts of several other minerals. Used often in Middle Eastern dishes such as hummus, salads, and stews.

Chiles - refers to peppers that vary greatly in size and heat. They range from 1/4-inch long to a foot long and from mildly warm to mouth blistering hot.
• Ancho - the ripened and dried form of the poblano chile. Has a deep red color and wrinkled skin.
• Chipotle - a jalapeno pepper that has been ripened, dried and smoked. It is brown-red in color and often used to season soups and stews.
• Jalapeno pepper - smooth, dark-green bullet-shaped fresh pepper ranging from hot to very hot. Used in salsas, dips, soups, stews and casseroles.
• Poblano - a dark green pepper with relatively mild flavor and heat.

Chili garlic sauce - medium heat chile sauce with robust flavor. It is made with coarsely ground chilies and garlic.
Brand Recommendation: Lee Kum Lee

Cocoa powder (unsweetened) - cocoa beans are fermented, roasted, and ground into chocolate liquor. They are then pressed to remove most of the fat (cocoa butter) and ground again into cocoa powder. Dutch process cocoa has a richer, smoother chocolate flavor than slightly bitter, natural cocoa but is lower in antioxidants. Use cocoa powder in baked goods, in savory dishes such as chili, and as a decorative garnish. Three tablespoons of unsweetened cocoa powder plus 1 tablespoon of oil can be substituted for 1-ounce of unsweetened baker's chocolate. I like to mix dutch process and natural cocoa to intensify the chocolate flavor of cakes and cookies.

Coconut - white, sweet meat of fresh coconut. Flaked coconut is made up of longer and moister pieces and shredded coconut is made up of shorter, dried pieces. Use unsweetened coconut to avoid refined sugar. Coconut is high in protein, vitamins(folic acid and all B Vitamins), minerals(including calcium, magnesium, and potassium), and beneficial fats.

Coconut oil - multipurpose oil used for baking and frying, and topically to condition skin and hair. Refer to the "Oils" section in the introduction of the book for more information.
Brand Recommendation: Tropical Traditions and Nutiva

Coconut milk - a smooth, rich-flavored liquid used in soups, sauces, baked goods, curries, and desserts. Choose unsweetened coconut milk as opposed to sugar-laden cream of coconut. Store leftover coconut milk in ice cube trays and freeze, then transfer cubes to a resealable plastic bag. Remove as needed.

Cornstarch - a fine powder derived from the endosperm of the corn kernel. It is used for thickening sauces and puddings. It causes digestive problems or allergic reactions in some. Cornstarch can be replaced with an equal amount of arrowroot. Choose brands that use non-genetically modified corn.
Brand Recommendation: Rumford

Cooking spray - oil in aerosol cans to create a nonstick surface. Choose cooking sprays that contain olive oil or grapeseed oil. Use cooking spray to coat baking pans or skillets, or on top of foods to help them to become brown and crispy in the oven.

Cornmeal - white or yellow flour produced by stone-grinding or crushing corn. Stone-ground is higher in nutrition as it retains the germ of the corn. Crushing removes both the hull and the germ.

Couscous - semolina durum wheat formed into small pearls of pasta. It is quick cooking and versatile. Look for whole wheat couscous to increase fiber and nutrients.

Crisp-tender - vegetables cooked until just tender but still somewhat crunchy.

Daikon radish (Chinese radish) -a popular Asian root vegetable that looks like a white carrot. They have a hotter flavor than traditional radishes.

Dandy Blend: a healthful, instant herbal beverage. This delicious coffee replacement is made from dandelion root, chicory root and beetroot and contains over 50 trace minerals. It has a rich, smooth, coffee-flavored taste without caffeine or acidity. I enjoy drinking it hot with almond milk as a coffee replacement and I use it in baking to intensify the flavors in baked goods containing cocoa.

<u>Dates(dried)</u> - the dried fruit of the palm tree. They are sweet and sticky with a papery skin and contain one small seed. Dates are high in soluble and insoluble fiber, potassium, and iron and contain small amounts of several other vitamins. They can be stored in an airtight container for up to 6 months at room temperature or in the refrigerator for up to one year. Dates are delicious when chopped and added to muffins and cakes, on top of salads, or stuffed with a whole almond and goat cheese.

<u>Dredge</u> - to coat completely in a dry mixture.

<u>Edamame</u> - fresh soybeans available in the pods or shelled.

<u>Evaporated cane sugar(evaporated cane juice)</u> - a straw colored raw sugar made from fresh cane juice. It is unrefined and naturally evaporated and crystallized. It retains the original natural vitamins and minerals. Use in moderation as it is still sugar. Refer to the "Sweeteners" section of the introduction for more information.
Brand Recommendation: Wholesome Sweeteners and Hain Pure Foods

<u>Evaporated skim milk</u> - creamy, thick milk made by evaporating half of the water from fresh skim milk. It is used in sauces, pudding, and pies.

<u>Extra virgin olive oil</u> - monounsaturated oil obtained from the first pressing of olives. It has a delicate flavor and is high in antioxidants. It is a light and healthful addition to salads, pasta , fish, and many other foods.

<u>Fennel</u> - a crunchy and slightly sweet vegetable. It is made up of a white or pale green bulb and stalks that are topped with feathery green leaves. Flowers grow near the leaves and produce fennel seeds.

<u>Feta cheese</u> - sharp, white crumbly cheese. It is traditionally made from sheep's or goat's milk but is often made from cow's milk in the United States.

<u>Flaxseeds (common flax/linseed)</u> - seeds of the flax plant. These highly nutritious seeds are a rich source of omega-3 fatty acids, fiber, and lignans (a compound connected to the prevention of some types of cancer). It stabilizes blood sugar, enhances your immune system, and helps to maintain a well functioning digestive tract. Use whole or ground in breads and muffins.

<u>Flaxseed meal</u> - ground flaxseeds. Both whole and ground flaxseeds are beneficial, however, the fat benefits are only available from flaxseed meal. The omega-3 oils in flaxseeds turn rancid quickly so grind whole seeds just prior to use, if possible. Store in the refrigerator or freezer.

<u>Fork-tender</u> - vegetables cooked until they can be pierced with a fork but are not mushy.

<u>Ghee</u> - clarified butter that is made by simmering unsalted butter until the water boils off and the milk solids settle to the bottom. The clarified butter is then separated from the solids. It has a high smoke point (it does not burn easily), a long shelf life, and does not need to be refrigerated. It is non-hydrogenated and has a long history of use in East Indian culture.

<u>Ginger</u> -a knobby, fibrous root with a smooth, light brown skin and pale, golden flesh. Fresh ginger has a pungent and slightly hot flavor and is great for stir-fries and marinades. Powdered ginger has a hot-sweet flavor and is used for gingerbread and pumpkin pie. Its taste is only slightly similar to fresh ginger so the two are not interchangeable. Ginger is great for digestion and nausea and is a natural antibiotic to battle colds.

<u>Gomasio</u> - dry roasted sesame seeds ground with mineral rich sea salt. Sesame oil coats the salt which reduces the harshness. It is a delicious table condiment as a replacement for table salt.
Brand Recommendation: Eden Organic

<u>Greek style yogurt</u> - thick, rich, and creamy yogurt with a variety of uses. It can replace sour cream in recipes or can be mixed with honey and used in place of whipped cream on top of desserts. If you don't have Greek yogurt, make yogurt cheese or use full-fat organic yogurt.

<u>Grapeseed oil</u> - a polyunsaturated fat derived from the seeds of grapes. It has a light and nutty yet neutral flavor and will not cloud when chilled. It has a high smoke point so it good for frying. It is also useful in baking, and making salad dressings. The oil is high in flavonoids (known to protect the heart), antioxidants, and linoleic acid (Omega-6). Use in the place of canola oil and store in the refrigerator.

<u>Immersion Blender(hand blender/stick blender)</u> - a kitchen appliance to blend or puree ingredients in the container in which they are being prepared.

<u>Jicama</u> - large round tuberous vegetable that is similar to a turnip is appearance. The flesh is sweet, watery, and crunchy. It does not become soggy after cutting so it makes a nice addition to salads, vegetable platters, and stir-fries.

<u>Kamut pasta</u> - a highly nutritious pasta made from kamut, an ancient high protein wheat. It does not have the heavy taste and texture of some whole wheat pastas. You can substitute brown rice pasta or whole grain pasta in recipes.
Brand Recommendation: Eden Organics

Lecithin - comes in liquid or granular form. It emulsifies cholesterol in the blood, regulates the deposit of fat in the liver, and breaks up fats into small particles. It is used in baking to give baked goods texture and moisture.

Lentils - high-protein and quick-cooking legumes. Lentils do not need to soak before cooking. Brown and red lentils become soft when cooked and French lentils tend to remain firm and nutty. Use in soups, salads, and stews. One cup of raw lentils yields 3 cups cooked.

Maple syrup - concentrated sap of the maple tree. Use real maple syrup as opposed to artificially flavored.

Mirin - a sweet Asian wine brewed from sweet brown rice. Used in salad dressings, marinades, and sauces.

Miso paste - fermented soybean paste. It is high in protein and probiotic enzymes that aid in digestion and improve intestinal flora. There is a wide variety ranging from mild white miso to dark hatcho miso. White miso has a very mild, lightly sweet flavor, yellow is a little saltier and stronger than white, red is stronger than yellow and best suited for winter soups, and dark brown or black has a very strong flavor and smell. The intensity of flavor depends on how long the miso was aged.

Mushrooms - a fleshy edible fungus that usually has a stem and a flattened cap. There are more than 2500 varieties. They are available fresh, canned, dried, and frozen. When using dried mushrooms, soak in hot water for 10 minutes then drain and rinse for use in soups and stews. Refrigerate fresh mushrooms in paper bags. 1 pound fresh mushrooms=6 cups sliced mushrooms=3-ounces dried mushrooms
+ Cremini - closely related to the white button mushroom but are slightly more flavorful. Large creminis are called portobello mushrooms.
+ Enoki - flower-like mushroom with a mild, light flavor. They grow in clusters and have long, slender stems and tiny caps.
+ Oyster - smooth texture and subtle oyster-like flavor. They are widely available and are great in soups and stir-fries.
+ Portobello - larger, hardier version of the white mushroom with a dense, meat-like flavor and texture. They can grown up to 6-inches in diameter and can be added to soups and stews, or can be grilled or stuffed.
+ Shiitake - large and meaty mushrooms that have the earthiness and flavor of wild mushrooms. They work well in stir-fries and soups.
+ White or Button - vary in color from creamy white to light brown and in size from small (button) to jumbo.

<u>Napa cabbage (Chinese cabbage)</u> - football-shaped, mild-tasting cabbage with crinkled leaves. Can be cooked or eaten raw.

<u>Nuts</u> - good source of protein. When eaten in moderate amounts, nuts can reduce the risk of heart disease, cancer, and type 2 diabetes.
- <u>Almonds</u> -high in calcium, Vitamin E. Although they contain a high amount of omega-6 fatty acids, they are still beneficial due to their heart disease and cancer preventing properties.
- <u>Pecan</u> - also high in omega-6 fatty acids but can help to prevent heart disease and cancer.
- <u>Walnuts</u> -considered one of the healthiest nuts to eat due to their high content of omega-3 fatty acids. Refer to the Oils section of the Introduction for the benefits of omega-3 fatty acids.

<u>Oats</u> - a very nutritious, hardy grain high in nutrients and soluble fiber. Oats are a great breakfast food. They stabilize blood sugar and keep you full and satisfied. TIP: Add a dash of salt to the water when cooking oatmeal to enhance the flavor.
- <u>Oat Flour</u> - powdered oats. Used in baking . Oat flour is low in gluten and is often combined with wheat flour when making leavened bread. Make your own oat flour by pulverizing rolled oats on high speed in a blender.
- <u>Quick Oats (also called quick-cooking oatmeal, easy oats)</u>- processed and steamed. They are like rolled oats but are cut finely before rolling. They cook in 3-4 minutes.
- <u>Rolled Oats (also called old-fashioned oats, oat flakes)</u>- oat groats that have been steamed, rolled, and flaked. They are more nutritious and chewier than quick oats. Used to make granola, muesli and cookies.

<u>Panko</u> - Light, crispy, coarse-ground, and crunchy Japanese style bread crumbs. They are excellent for breading and fillers as they tend to stay crispy longer than regular bread crumbs and absorb less grease.

<u>Phyllo dough</u> - paper-thin sheets of wheat dough used for making flaky pies, Greek spanakopita, and strudels. It is available in the frozen section of supermarkets. Health food stores also usually carry a whole wheat phyllo.

<u>Prunes</u> - dried plums. They have a sweet taste and a sticky, chewy texture. Prunes are high in antioxidants, potassium, and soluble fiber and increase the body's ability to absorb iron.

<u>Puree</u> - to blend foods until smooth, using a blender or food processor.

<u>Raw honey</u> - honey that is not heated or filtered, therefore retains healthful minerals, vitamins, enzymes, and amino acids. Traces of the pollen, propolis, and beeswax collect

at the top and can be eaten or scraped off. Raw honey varies in color from almost white to golden brown. It has traditionally been used as a remedy for seasonal allergies. It is high in enzymes that aid digestion and long term benefits include a strong immune system and increased respiratory health. Eat raw honey on bread, in salad dressing, or in sauces to retain beneficial nutrients.

Saute - to cook food quickly in a small amount of fat.

Sea salt - seawater dried by the sun or wind or vacuum-dried at low temperatures. It retains all sea water minerals.

Semolina flour - high-protein and high-gluten flour made from durum wheat. It is ideal for making pasta and is occasionally used in breads and baked goods. A small amount adds nice texture to baked goods. Semolina flour gives bread a crispy crust and chewy interior. I use it in the Honey Whole Grain Bread recipe.

Sesame Oil - oil extracted from sesame seeds. There are 2 varieties, light and dark. The light has a subtle flavor and a high smoke point. It is ideal for stir-frying. Dark sesame oil (toasted sesame oil) is extracted from toasted sesame seeds. It has a nutty flavor and aroma. It is used in salad dressings, marinades, and as a flavoring agent after the dish is cooked. When heated, dark sesame oil loses its flavor and burns easily so it is not used as a cooking oil.

Shoyu - traditionally aged soy sauce. It is made from soy, wheat, water, and salt. It has a bright, fresh taste.

Simmer - to cook bubbling liquid over low heat.

Soy milk - made by extracting liquid from soybeans that have been soaked, ground, boiled, and pressed dry. Available in a variety of flavors. Taste differs greatly from brand to brand.

Stevia glycerite - a slightly thickened alcohol-free version of stevia. It also contains vegetable glycerine and water. It is my favorite stevia to use. I leaves no bitter or licorice aftertaste and a little goes a long way. Refer to the "Sweeteners" section of the introduction for more information.
Brand Recommendation. NOW Foods

Sucanat - a contraction of sugar cane natural. It is non-refined cane sugar that retains its molasses content. Substitute for equal amounts for brown sugar.

<u>Sunflower Seeds</u> - seeds from the sunflower. They are high in magnesium, calcium, phosphorus, and unsaturated fats.

<u>Sweet red chili sauce</u> - a versatile, medium-heat sweet and savory sauce made form sun-ripened chile peppers and garlic. Serve as a dipping sauce for spring rolls, grilled meats, or vegetables; often used in salad dressings.

<u>Tamari</u> - a sauce made primarily from soybeans. It is similar to soy sauce but is thicker and has a smoother and more complex flavor. It can be used instead of soy sauce in cooking, or as a table condiment.

<u>Tahini</u> - sesame seed paste originating from the Middle East. The most flavorful tahini is made from toasted sesame seeds. It is used in making dips and salad dressings. Available in traditional grocery stores, health food stores, and Middle Eastern markets.
Brand Recommendations: Arrowhead Mills, Goya, Marantha

<u>Tofu(bean curd)</u> - a soybean product available in white blocks. It is available in a variety of degrees of firmness from silken to extra firm. It is bland on its own but readily absorbs seasonings and marinades.

<u>Unbleached all purpose flour</u> - white flour that is not chemically processed or bleached. White flour has been stripped of all its nutrients. I use it occasionally to give baked goods a lighter texture.

<u>Vinegar</u> - a sour liquid obtained by converting a fermented liquid to a weak acetic acid solution. Used as a preservative or as a condiment. Vinegar will keep indefinitely when kept in a cool, dark place.

- <u>Apple cider vinegar</u> - a strong, zesty, cleansing, healing, energizing vinegar made from apples. Also referred to as "cider vinegar". Use in salad dressings, marinades, and drinks. Use raw, unfiltered vinegar if available.
  Brand Recommendation. Bragg
- <u>Balsamic vinegar</u> - a popular vinegar made from grape pressings and aged for varied amounts of time in wooden kegs. It has a rich, slightly sweet, robust flavor. It is great for salad dressings, sauces, and drizzled over fresh strawberries or raspberries. The taste will differ based on the quality of the vinegar.
- <u>Brown rice vinegar</u> - vinegar made from brown rice. It has a mellow flavor and low acidity. Rice vinegar can be used in place of brown rice vinegar. . .
- <u>Distilled white vinegar</u> - made from a grain-alcohol mixture. It has a stronger taste than cider vinegar.
- <u>Rice vinegar</u> - made from fermented rice. It has a mild, slightly sweet taste.
- <u>Wine vinegar</u> - made from red or white wine.

Wasabi - Japanese horseradish. It has a fiery-hot flavor and comes as a light green powder. It is available in health food stores and Asian markets.

Watercress - one of the oldest known leaf vegetables. It has a peppery, tangy flavor. Use in salads and sandwiches or as a garnish.

Wheat bran (Miller's bran) - the outer layer of wheat. It is packed with nutrition, high in fiber, protein, and several minerals and vitamins. Purchase wheat bran in bulk and add to baked goods and pancakes.

Wheat germ - a small part of the wheat kernel. It contains more nutrition per ounce than any other vegetable or grain. Wheat germ is very high in protein and contains several minerals and vitamins (including high amounts of Vitamins B and E). Add nutrition to baked goods and pancakes by replacing up to 1/4 cup flour with wheat germ. Store in the refrigerator or freezer.

Whole wheat pastry flour - a flour similar to white pastry flour, however, it retains the bran and germ portions of the kernel. It has a fine texture and high starch content. Due to its low gluten content, it is not used in baking bread. This flour is a staple in my kitchen. It is my favorite flour to use in all baked goods except yeast breads. It is higher in nutrition than white flour but does not have a heavy, whole wheat taste and texture. To retain freshness, store in the refrigerator or freezer.

Whole wheat flour - flour that is ground from the full wheat berry. It has high levels of protein, fiber, iron, as well as several vitamins and minerals. Due to the presence of the wheat germ, the shelf life is shorter. It is best to store whole wheat flour in the fridge or freezer. Using whole wheat flour alone in baking bread results in a nutritious but dense product. It helps to use both unbleached bread flour or all-purposed flour and whole wheat flour. To retain freshness, store in the refrigerator or freezer.

Wonton wrappers - square or round sheets of wheat dough. Available in the refrigerated section of grocery stores, health food stores, and Asian markets. They will keep for about a week in the fridge or a few months in the freezer.

Xanthan gum - a microbial polysaccharide derived from Xanthomonas campestris and produced from the cellulose of cabbage. It is used in dairy products and salad dressings and acts as a natural stabilizer or thickener similar to gelatin. It prevents ice crystals from forming in ice creams and provides no-fat dairy products with a texture similar to a full-fat products. Use 1/8 teaspoon per cup of liquid. Mix in a blender instead of by hand, as it clumps easily. Can be purchased at health food stores and online.

Yogurt cheese - thick, creamy yogurt that can replace sour cream or cream cheese in recipes. You can make it out of low-fat or regular yogurt. To make yogurt cheese: line a strainer with cheesecloth and set it over a bowl. Spoon 32-ounces of yogurt in the colander and cover with plastic wrap. Refrigerate for 4 hours or overnight then discard the liquid that collects at the bottom of the bowl. It should have the consistency of soft cream cheese. Cover and keep in the fridge for up to a week.

Zest - the brightly flavored and colored rind of citrus fruits. An addition of a little amount of zest adds intense citrus flavor to a dish.

METRIC EQUIVALENTS

LIQUID MEASURES

U.S.	METRIC
1/4 teaspoon	1.25 milliliters
1/2 teaspoon	2.5 milliliters
1 teaspoon	5 milliliters
1 tablespoon	15 milliliters
1 fluid oz	30 milliliters
1/4 cup	60 milliliters
1/3 cup	80 milliliters
1/2 cup	125 milliliters
1 cup	250 milliliters
1 pint (2 cups)	500 milliliters
1 quart (4 cups)	960 milliliters
4–1/2 cups	1 liter
1 gallon (4 quarts)	3.84 liters

DRY MEASURES

U.S.	METRIC
1 oz	28 grams
4 oz (1/4 pound)	114 grams
8 oz (1/2 pound)	225 grams
16 oz (1 pound)	454 grams
2.2 pounds	1000 grams (1 kilogram)

OVEN-TEMPERATURE EQUIVALENCIES

FAHRENHEIT	CELSIUS	DESCRIPTION
200	90	Cool
250	120	Very Slow
325	170	Moderately Slow
350	180	Moderate
400	200	Moderately Hot
450	230	Hot
475	240	Extremely Hot

RESOURCES

Agave Nectar
Madhava
PO Box 756
Lyons, CO 80540

Brown Rice Syrup and Brown Rice
Lundberg Family Farms
PO Box 369
Richvale, CA 95974-0369
1-916-882-4551

Breads and Sprouted Tortillas
Food for Life Baking C. (Ezekial)
PO Box 1434
Corona, CA 91718-1434
1-800-797-5090

Alvarado Street Bakery
2225 S. McDowell Blvd
Petaluma, CA 94954
(707)283-0300

Brown Rice Syrup, Pasta, and Condiments

Eden Organics
701 Tecumseh
Clinton, Michigan 49236
424-3336
HYPERLINK "mailto:info@edenfoods.com" info@edenfoods.com

Chocolate, White Chocolate, and Peanut Butter Chips

Sunspire
San Leandro, CA 94577
(510)346-386. HYPERLINK "http://www.sunspire.com" www.sunspire.com
Coffee-flavored beverage
Instant, herbal coffee-replacement

Dandy Blend
3283 Fairfax Road
Cleveland, Ohio 44118
(800)697-485. http://www.dandyblend.com

Coconut Oil

Nutiva
PO Box 1716
Sebastopol, CA 95473
1-800-993-436. HYPERLINK "http://www.nutiva.com"
www.nutiva.com

Tropical Traditions
POB 333
Springville, CA 9326. HYPERLINK "http://www.tropicaltraditions.com"
www.tropicaltraditions.com

Natural Meat Produts

100% preservative, additive, hormone and antibiotic free turkey, beef and pork products

Wellshire Farms
509 Woodstown Rd.
Swedesboro, NJ 08085
(856)769-893. www.wellshirefarms.com

Applegate Farms
750 Route 202 South, Third Floor
Bridgewater, NJ 08807
1-866-587-585. HYPERLINK "http://www.applegatefarms.com"
www.applegatefarms.com

Milk Alternatives

Almond Breeze
- almond milk available in sweetened and unsweetened original, vanilla and chocolate
Blue Diamond Growers
Sacramento, C. 9581. HYPERLINK "http://www.bluediamond.com"
www.bluediamond.com

Pacific Natural Food.
-available in several varieties of nut and grain beverages
Tualatin, OR 97062
1-503-692-966. HYPERLINK "http://www.pacificfoods.com" www.pacificfoods.com

Shoyu (traditionally brewed soy sauce)

San-J International, Inc.
2880 Sprouse Dr.
Richmond, Virginia 23231
1-800-446-550.
HYPERLINK "http://www.san-j.com" www.san-j.com

Stevia
Natural, non-glycemic sweetener

NOW (Nutrition for Optimal Wellness) Foods
Bloomingdale, IL 6010.
HYPERLINK "http://www.nowfoods.com" www.nowfoods.com
- manufacturers of vitamins, minerals, dietary supplements, and natural foods. They offer high quality products at competitive prices. They carry several types of stevia including Stevia Glycerite, powdered extracts and liquid drops (plain and flavored)

Steviva Brands, Inc.
725 NW Flanders St. Suite 402
Portland, OR 9720. (310)455-987.
www.steviva.com
- an environmentally responsible company dedicated to bringing customers the finest quality products available. Their products are GMO, gluten, and chemical free and they use a pure water extraction process. They offer powdered
stevia extract, Steviva Blend, and Fructevia.
Steviva Blend is a mixture of stevia powder and natural erythritol. It is similar in sweetness and consistency to sugar and is great for baking and cooking. It replaces sugar 2:1.
Fructevia is a blend of Fructose, FOS, and stevia. Fructose is a natural, low-glycemic (20) fruit sugar and FOS(fructooligosaccharide) is a "pre-biotic" that supports intestinal health. It replaces sugar 2:1.

SweetLeaf Stevia Plus
Wisdom Natural Brands
1203 W. San Pedro St.
Gilbert, AZ 85233
1-800-899-990.

HYPERLINK "http://www.wisdomnaturalsbrands.com"
www.wisdomnaturalsbrands.com
- manufacturers of stevia powder, tablets, and liquid drops (plain and flavored)
The stevia plants are dried and concentrated using purified water only.
They have high quality products with no bitter aftertaste.

Sugars

Wholesome Sweeteners
Organic brown sugar, evaporated cane sugar,
agave nectar, Sucanat, and powdered sugar

SugarLand,
TX 77478
(800) 680-189.
HYPERLINK "http://www.OrganicSugars.biz" www.OrganicSugars.biz

Hain Pure Foods
-a variety of products from sugars and sea salt to crackers and oils
Hain Celestial Group, Inc.
Uniondale, NY 11553
434-4246

Tahini and Nut Butters
Arrowhead Mills (see below)

Marantha
tahini and a variety of nut butters
(510)346-386.
HYPERLINK "http://www.maranthanutbutters.com" www.maranthanutbutters.com

Thickeners and Leaveners

Bob's Red Mill Natural Foods, Inc.
Arrowroot, Xanthan Gum, and aluminum-free baking powder and baking soda
5209 SE International Way
Milwaukie, OR 97222
1-800-553-225.
HYPERLINK "http://www.bobredmill.com" www.bobsredmill.com

Rumford
Baking powder and cornstarch (made with non-GMO corn)
Clabber Girl Corporation
Terre Haute, IN 4780
HYPERLINK "http://www.rumfordworld.com"
www.rumfordworld.com

Whole Grain Flours

Arrowhead Mills, Inc. / King Arthur Flour
Hereford, TX 7904 PO Box 876
1-800-749-073 Norwich, VT 05055
1-800-827-6836

Whole Foods Market
-a natural foods and supplement company offering high quality natural and organic
foods and a commitment to sustainable agriculture.
www.wholefoodsmarket.com

Vitamin Cottage Stores
-offers natural health food and nutritional supplements at affordable everyday prices.
1-800-817-941. . www.vitamincottage.com

INDEX

A

B

P

Pancakes
- Banana Wheat Germ, 41
- Blueberry Wheat Germ, 41
- Oatmeal Raisin, 42
- Wheat Germ, 41

Parmesan Baked French Fries, 104
Parmesan Broccoli and Cauliflower, 96
Parmesan Potato Chunks, 106
Pasta Sauce, 191
Peach and Applesauce Cake, 164
Peach Applesauce Muffins, 164
Peach Muffins, 47
Peach Sauce, 45
Peanut Butter and Honey Cookies, 146
Pecans, see Nuts
Phyllo Spinach Pie, 100
Pie, Pumpkin with Gingersnap Crust, 172
Pilaf, Vegetable Quinoa, 107
Pilaf, Black Bean Quinoa, 107
Pineapple Burgers with Honey Barbeque Sauce, 90

Pita Chips
- Garlic, 23
- Parmesan, 23

Pizza Crust, Whole Wheat, 40

Potato
- Mixed Potato Chunks, 106
- Parmesan, Chunks, 106
- Overstuffed Baked, 80

Powdered Milk Frosting, 177
Pretzels, Honey Mustard, 29
Prune Puree, 183
Pumpkin Bread, 58
Pumpkin Carrot Jam Muffins, 52
Pumpkin Chocolate Chip Cookies, 149
Pumpkin Cheesecake Bars, 160
Pumpkin Cream Cheese Loaf, 55
Pumpkin Pie with Gingersnap Crust, 172
Pumpkin, Supermoist Cake, 167

Q

Quesadillas
- Chicken, 69
- Veggie, 31

Quinoa
- Pilaf, Black Bean, 107
- Pilaf, Vegetable, 107

R

Raw Spiced Almonds, 24
Refried Bean and Chicken Tostadas, 83
Rhuberry Crisp, 173
Roasted Asparagus, 97
Roasted Rosemary Vegetables, 95

S

Salads
- Asian, with Glazed Pan-Fried Tofu, 131
- Baby Spinach and Strawberry, 126
- BLT Pasta, 121
- Blue Cheese and Walnut, 126
- Carrot, Broccoli and Raisin, 125
- Chicken, Tomato and Basil Pasta, 122
- Creamy Curry Coleslaw, 130
- Cucumber and Watermelon, 132
- Curry Veggie Pasta, 123
- Goat Cheese and Cranberry, 127
- Green Bean Slaw, 128
- Grilled Vegetable Pasta, 120
- Jicama Coleslaw, 129
- Three Bean, 124

Salad Dressings
- Balsamic Vinaigrette, 134
- Carrot, 136
- Creamy Italian, 135
- French Tarragon, 137
- Honey Mustard, 136
- Honey Poppy Seed, 137
- Miso, 135

Salmon, Seared with Garlic Spinach and White Beans, 74
Salsa
-Fresh Garden, 188

White Chocolate Cherry Fudgy Cookies, 147
White Fluff Frosting, 176
White Wine Reduction, 62
Whole Grain Bagels, 39
Whole Grain Bagel Breadsticks, 39
Whole Wheat Crepes, 44
Whole Wheat French Toast, 43
Whole Wheat Pizza Crust, 40
Wontons
   - Edamame and Avocado, 34
   - Spinach and Cheese, 33
   - Spinach Feta, 33

X

Xanthan Gum, 134, 206

Y

Yellow Cake, 172
Yogurt Cream, Sweet, 160

Z

Zucchini Chips, 93
Zucchini, Chocolate Cake, 166
Zucchini Chocolate Chip Loaf, 56
Zucchini Oatmeal Muffins, 50
Zucchini Parmesan Casserole, 85
Zucchini Parmesan Quickbread, 37
Zucchini Pineapple Loaf, 56
Zucchini, Stuffed, 102